The Business of Conferences

The Business of Conferences

A hospitality sector overview for the UK and Ireland

Anton Shone

OXFORD BOSTON JOHANNESBURG MELBOURNE NEW DELHI SINGAPORE

Butterworth-Heinemann
Linacre House, Jordan Hill, Oxford OX2 8DP
225 Wildwood Avenue, Woburn, MA 01801-2041
A division of Reed Educational and Professional Publishing Ltd

 A member of the Reed Elsevier plc group

First published 1998

British Library Cataloguing in Publication Data
Shone, Anton
   The Business of conferences: a hospitality sector overview
   for the UK and Ireland
   1. Congresses and conventions – Planning   2. Hospitality industry –
   Great Britain   3. Hospitality industry – Ireland
   I. Title
   647.9'4'41

ISBN 0 7506 4099 5

Typeset by Avocet Typeset, Brill, Aylesbury, Bucks
Printed and bound in Great Britain by
Biddles Ltd, Guildford and King's Lynn

Contents _____

Part Two: Facilities and Services

Part Three: Management Issues

Preface

Conferencing forms a large part of the UK economy, perhaps as much as seven billion pounds a year, and makes a significant contribution to the economy of Ireland, though this latter is more difficult to quantify. The conference business has not, until comparatively recently, attracted the significant attention of researchers and writers. The purpose of this book is to provide a foundation for those wishing to study the conference business. It is hoped the framework provided here will act as a jumping off point for further study, and as such, will pique the interest of students, teachers, researchers and practitioners alike, to explore the subject further. The shelves of any library provide numerous texts on 'How to run a conference' but very little about how the conference business operates and is managed, or how conferencing can be seen as an economic and social activity.

I am extremely grateful for the contributions made to the drafts of the book by a range of people, including Bryn Parry and David McCaskey of the Colchester Institute; for the views expressed by practitioners in the conference industry about the skills that contemporary students need, particularly staff of the Brewery Conference Centre in London, the International Convention Centre in Birmingham, Hayley Conference Centres at Little Horwood and Cranage Hall, and the staff and managements of Principal Hotels, DeVere Hotels and Mount Charlotte Thistle Hotels. I am also most grateful to James O'Neill of the Inntel Conference Agency and his staff at Marks Tey, near Colchester, for their kind help. I would also wish to express my most grateful thanks to Dr Denis Harrington of the Waterford Institute of Technology and to the Convention Bureau of Ireland.

I am also extremely grateful to the two Pennys, experts at word processing both, for their efforts and patience on my behalf. This book is by no means definitive and I urge the reader to bear that in mind and to use it as a starting place. Any comments readers may wish to make will be gladly received.

Anton Shone
Clacton on Sea

Part One —————————————

The Conference Business ————

1

The evolution and extent of the conference business

The aims of this chapter are:

1 To consider a brief history of trade in Britain and Ireland with specific reference to the conference business and to examine the developments which have resulted in the modern industry.
2 To examine the social and economic significance of the conference business.
3 To discuss the extent and scope of the conference business in seasonal and geographic terms.

1.1 Introduction

The conference business is a major contributor to the economy in terms of the benefits it brings. These benefits range from the provision of employment to the income from foreign conference delegates visiting both Britain and Ireland. The history of the conference business is chiefly one of great expansion within the past 30 years and to a lesser extent during the previous 250 years, beginning with the creation of assembly rooms in spa towns. Today the industry is a multi-million pound business, but it is not generally perceived as separate, as its fortunes are bound up with that of the hospitality and tourism industry, which provides both in-house conference facilities and also, in hotels, bedroom accommodation for other conference centres.

The impacts on a local community of a major conference centre, be it purpose built, or be it as part of some local hotel provision, can be perceived in terms of the local economic multiplier (Braun and

Rungeling, 1992). A conference centre itself may not, for example, provide huge direct employment, but the indirect effects on local businesses, local services and local infrastructure and environment are extremely significant. These indirect effects may include the support of activities such as retailing (conference delegates buying anything from magazines to clothing) and catering (conference delegates using restaurants, coffee shops and pubs outside the main centre) to less obvious support in terms of services such as transport, taxis, advertising, technical equipment supplies and so on.

The conference business is, to some extent, regional, in so far as the biggest concentrations of demand are in London and the Midlands in Britain, and Dublin in Ireland. This demand is facilitated by good transport networks – rail, air and road nets; by the provision of hotels and other forms of accommodation of a high standard; and by the provision of adequate venues themselves. A number of large, purpose-built venues have been opened to cope with this demand, but it is significant to point out that the conference business is highly competitive locally, regionally and nationally.

1.2   History of the conference business

It would be easy to consider the conference business as a 'recent' phenomenon in Britain and Ireland, that is to say, a product of the industrial revolution and the need for the greater interchange of ideas. However, this would ignore some 2000 years of recorded civilization, and would wrongly suppose that trade, commercial interaction and debate had not taken place. Trade, interaction and debate did take place and, even on its modest scale, was as important in the basilicas, forums and inns of Roman Britain and the royal raths of Ireland as it is now, in purpose-built conference centres, hotels and inns.

Roman-British society and trade (AD 43–410) was vastly different from those we take for granted today. The evolution of meeting places reflects this. Few people in ancient times travelled far from their birthplace and business was conducted on a smaller and more intimate scale than in our modern world, via a network of personal friends, relatives and acquaintances. In Britain, the centre of activity for business and meeting was the Basilica (public hall) and the Forum (market place). From the first century AD, the cities of Roman Britain all had such places and in the provincial capitals of Cirencester, London, Lincoln and York, these were of considerable importance. Merchants displayed their goods, information and news were exchanged and visitors introduced by local people. In as much as this was true of the provincial capitals, it was also true of the other great cities and towns. From Carlisle in the north to Exeter in the south, from Chester in the west to Colchester in the east, all possessed such buildings, though trade and exchange also took place in taverns and temples. Roman civilization in Britain did not end abruptly, as it had in other parts of the Roman empire after 410, but endured a long slow decline. In some cities, such as King Arthur's Camelot (i.e. Colchester 475–515) and Wroxeter, new buildings, found by archaeological evidence, suggest that urban civilization long endured before succumbing to the more agricultural society of the Saxon period and early middle ages (Morris, 1995a).

Ireland, the Romans did not conquer. Trade existed, however, and this took place on much the same intimate and local scale as it did in the provincial towns of Roman Britain. The great kings of Ireland, from Tuathal onwards, also encouraged trade and the exchange of merchandise. The splendour and peace with which some of the Irish kings reigned, such as Cormac: 'obsolutely the best king that ever Raigned in Ireland before himselfe' (218–256), as a chronicler gently recorded him, and later, at the time of King Arthur in Britain, King Mac Erca in Ireland (Morris, 1995b), saw a great expansion in the activities of merchants and traders. However, after Diarmaid and his conflict with Columba, then abbot of Derry, in 560, the power of the high kings weakened and Christianity took a stronger role in Irish society. The Vikings, invading in 795, began to build walled towns, including Dublin, Wexford, Waterford, Cork and Limerick. This development started to create a society not unlike that of the Saxon period in England, and just as Alfred the Great fought the Danes to a standstill in Wessex, so too did the last of the great Irish high kings, Brian Boru, at the Battle of Clontarf in 1014.

Although the society of the early middle ages in Saxon England and Christian Ireland was predominantly rural and feudal, merchants travelled and goods were traded. Trade often took place in churches, which acted as meeting places and community centres. In England during the reign of King Edgar (949–975) Canon 26 forbade drinking in churches – this was not so much a reflection of blasphemy, but a recognition that churches were meeting places and could become rowdy. After the defeat of the last Saxon king (Harold II) at Hastings in 1066, trade continued to evolve slowly with commerce then beginning to centre on market towns. The Normans began their rule in England by constructing huge castles to subdue the Saxon population. They then expanded this policy to Ireland in 1169, though with less success and much conflict.

Merchants and local people met to trade, exchange news and information and convert goods into cash. Market towns gradually became more important and communications between them, i.e. roads, were improved. The Statute of Winchester (1285) required that highways between market towns be enlarged and 'cleared for 200 yards' on each side to discourage robbery. Throughout the middle ages market towns remained important. Trade developed and so did the specialization of trading roles – goldsmiths, for example, became bankers. Towns sought to increase their importance by holding fairs and the medieval merchant guilds sought to control trade in their businesses. The City of London had a number of guilds (sometimes called livery companies) with their own guild halls where their members met, often as a 'court' to determine issues of trade (Clout, 1991). In other towns, the merchant guilds held great fairs to attract people to the town for trade and meetings. Preston guild fair, held once every 20 years, survives to this day, as do others, such as Nottingham Goose Fair, an annual event.

Guild halls took over the role of churches as trade meeting places. In York, the Guildhall (c. 1370), St Anthony's Hall, the Merchant Taylor's Hall and the Merchant Adventurer's Hall are all surviving examples of this role, though inns continued to sustain informal gatherings, and meetings of merchants and traders. By the late 1500s, during the reign of Elizabeth I, and throughout the 1600s, inns became more important to trade and commerce, and as meeting places. However, from the mid-1650s, coffee houses began to develop as places to exchange news and to trade. By 1688, Lloyds Coffee House had become the meeting place for London's shippers and marine insurers and much the same was true of other coffee houses, where bankers, lawyers and other professional people began to meet. The same general pattern took place in Ireland, more so in Dublin, where the Georgian period saw an unparalleled spate of building (Bramah, 1972; Doran et al. 1992). Although very different from today's conference venue, the common feature of meetings in these locations to undertake trade is clear.

Prior to the industrial revolution, the development of fashionable Georgian towns such as Bath, Buxton and Cheltenham provided an impetus for the creation of major public buildings, including assembly rooms. While these were chiefly places of public entertainment, they also provided for the meeting and congregation of the merchant and professional classes (Girouard, 1990). This was also the case with public buildings in the larger cities of the period, such as the Assembly Rooms in York, built in 1736 by the Earl of Burlington, and those in Dublin, built by Dr Mosse in Parnell Square, now the Gate Theatre. In London, rooms for public assembly could be found not only in some of the larger and more obvious locations such as Guildhall, in the coffee houses of the time, and in the exchanges (the Stock Exchange, the Baltic Mercantile and Shipping Exchange etc.) then being built or extended, but also, of course, at the inns. The greater inns of this period had 'long rooms' which, given the development of many inns from monastic hostels, were places for a company of people to meet. By the end of the eighteenth century some of these 'long rooms' had become both assembly room and ballroom, many being as ornate and glittering as the assembly rooms of the spa towns (Bruning and Paulin, 1982)

For the purpose of the dissemination of knowledge, there were places of assembly in the older universities such as Oxford, Cambridge, Durham, St Andrews and Trinity College, though these were not commonly 'public'. Rooms could be found for public meeting purposes in some of the scientific societies such as the Royal Society, Royal Geographic Society and the Royal Society for the Encouragement of Arts (1754) in London and the Royal Irish Academy in Dublin. As the industrial revolution developed in the early 1800s, the need for places to conduct trade and commerce increased. Some of this trade and commerce took place in town halls, many of which continue in use today as venues for conferences and, of course, entertainment. Following the expansion of the Georgian spa towns of the 1700s into the Victorian resorts of the 1800s (Burkart and Medlik, 1981), the concept of the assembly room was often the precursor of the development of buildings such as 'Winter Gardens' and 'Floral Halls'. These buildings, while intended for leisure purposes, were also suitable venues for assembly and a number of them pre-dated the construction of large exhibition halls associated with the need to show off Victorian engineering skills. The most famous of these latter is probably Crystal Palace, built to house the Great Exhibition of 1851 and later destroyed by fire (1936), a similar fate having overtaken the Bingley Hall in Birmingham. Exhibitions were not the sole reason behind the creation of large halls. There was a growing demand by the middle of the Victorian period for venues for meetings, which was satisfied by the creation of a number of specialist assembly and banqueting locations such as the Cafe Royal and the Connaught Rooms in London and the Shelbourne Hotel in Dublin.

Then, as now, however, most meetings were rather small affairs and many were handled by the inns and hotels of the day. Throughout the nineteenth century the principal hotels tended to be run by the railway companies, though with a few masters of the industry, of whom Frederick Gordon was the greatest, running their own companies (Taylor, 1977). Just about anything with the title 'Grand' or 'Metropole' would serve to denote a major Victorian hotel, examples being the Midland Grand at St Pancras and in Manchester, and others such as those in Brighton, Birmingham, Scarborough, Leicester or Clacton (Shaw and Williams, 1997). Indeed, any Victorian town worth its salt could boast a 'Grand' hotel. In so far as such hotels provided accommodation, food and drink to travellers, they also provided rooms for assembly or 'congress', as the Victorians would have called it, ranging from small meeting rooms to the vast and opulent ballrooms of the day.

After 1900, however, it was possible to see a change in the demand for meetings. Though assemblies and congresses continued to be driven by trade and industry, there was a slow and gradual increase in activity which, rather than promoting products, or reporting a company's annual progress, looked to developing staff and sales. The precursors of the sales training meeting, the 'congress of commercials' (or commercial travellers) of the 1920s and 1930s, began to develop into something more modern and more recognizable. The beginnings of other types of conference activity were also discernible: with improvements in transport, and particularly the beginnings of commercial air travel between the two world wars, there was a perceptible, though initially small, development of the international conference. The conference trade itself continued to expand after each world war, though more slowly in Ireland, preoccupied by independence after 1921, but in particular from 1945 onwards. By the 1960s, the conference trade was recognizable as a significant part of the turnover of hotels and a number of public venues.

As had been the case with the railway companies during the Victorian period, airline companies such as Pan American and Trans World Airways sought to develop hotels, being concerned that the growth in air transport provision might outstrip the hotel supply. This, together with, in Britain, the Hotel Development Incentive Scheme of 1969, saw a rapid expansion in hotel provision (and thus meeting room provision). Related to the growth of international air

travel, there was a concomitant decline in holiday taking in domestic resorts; this pushed a number of the major resorts into considering how to ensure their economic stability and resulted in the
opening of the first major purpose-built civic conference venues in
the UK, good examples being those in Brighton (1977), Harrogate
(1982) and Bournemouth (1984). The development of major civic
venues continued sporadically throughout the 1970s and 1980s cul-
minating in the construction of several very large purpose-built
centres in major cities in the UK during the 1990s, including the
International Convention Centre (ICC) in Birmingham and the
Scottish Exhibition and Conference Centre in Glasgow. In total,
there are about 30 major centres of this kind in the UK now, which
could be described as the front rank of conference centre development. It is very important to bear in mind, however, that such
centres probably account for less than 5 per cent of provision. Total
provision can be classified into several groups, of which the largest
single group is hotels, accounting for 77 per cent of venues (Coopers
and Lybrand Deloitte, 1990). See Chapter 3 for an analysis. The
classification of conference venues which we will use can be found in
Figure 1.1.

Purpose-built conference centres

Municipal multi-purpose centres

Residential conference centres and in-company facilities

Academic venues

Hotels:

- De luxe city centre hotels
- Country house hotels
- other hotels

Unusual venues

Figure 1.1   Types of conference centre

Some 2000 years of recorded history have been skimmed in a few
short paragraphs. Trade and commerce have continued in many
forms during those 2000 years. Meetings held for the purpose of
trade have also continued, whether in markets or inns, churches or
assembly rooms. Nevertheless, the modern world is vastly different

from that of AD 100. Conference centres are largely a modern phenomenon, a product of changes in trade, commerce and communication during the past 30 to 40 years. A Roman Briton of AD 100 or
a chamberlain of Cormac's court would probably easily recognize a
market (at least an open air one) were he or she transported by a
miracle to today, but the modern conference centre would probably
mean less, except as a place of assembly. Nevertheless, the conference business is huge and significant; important in both social and
economic terms.

1.3   The social and economic significance

Social significance

Conferencing can be seen as part of business travel, within the
framework of the tourism industry. The industry comprises a
number of elements, the principal ones being the availability of
attractions, the provision of transport, the availability of accommodation, food and drink, and the provision of infrastructure and
support services. For a town or city wishing to become a destination
for business travellers, or more specifically, conference delegates,
these elements must be present. In looking back at the historical
development of some of the major conference destinations, it can be
seen that all four elements are present. This has been the case particularly for resort and spa towns such as Brighton or Harrogate. A
purpose-built conference centre would be constructed as a public (or
private) project in much the same way as the assembly rooms of the
Georgian period were (Girouard, 1990) and was often intended to
build on existing elements such as good transport networks (by road
or rail); the availability of good local accommodation (hotels) and
places of refreshment (restaurants and cafés); also attractions such as
a pleasant location, warm climate or tourist attraction in or near the
town. In the case of recent developments, the design provided may
be several elements put together as a package (the Birmingham ICC
having not only a convention area, but also an adjacent hotel and
retail area). Law (1993) clearly develops this discussion in the light
of the more general aspects of urban tourism and notes that 'in some
cities up to 40 per cent of those staying overnight in serviced
accommodation have come from this type of ... tourism'. As a consequence, many towns, cities and resorts have seen the conference
business as their economic salvation when other forms of tourism,

such as vacation tourism or heritage tourism might not be appropriate to their area. A number of conference centre developments have been undertaken on this economic basis, and while conference centres themselves may not, for example, employ large numbers of people, they nevertheless, in Law's view, have a wide impact on employment in the vicinity.

This is not to say that the development of a conference centre is the correct solution to the economic problems of any town, city or resort. If a public body, such as a city council, invests in a conference centre it must naturally forego investing in something else, say an industrial or retail development or better local housing. There is an opportunity cost. In considering the possibilities for the economic regeneration of an area, the construction of a conference centre is only one option, not a panacea. Loftman and Nevin (1992) clearly make this point in relation to the ICC in Birmingham. The opportunity cost was that of employment foregone because of the need to finance the debt incurred on the capital cost of the development. As they might say in Birmingham – you pay your money and you take your choice. (After a careful financial feasibility study, of course.)

Economic significance

A major comprehensive survey of the UK conference market published by Coopers and Lybrand Deloitte (1990) suggested that the market was worth 'considerably in excess of £6 billion' and reported over 115 million delegate days. It is impossible to provide an accurate update of the figures without further research data, and satisfactory comprehensive research has not been carried out since, though a number of other surveys do exist, including the '1996 Key Note Exhibitions and Conferences Market Sector Overview Report' and the annual surveys of the Meetings Industry Association. Unfortunately, none of these surveys appear comparable, and this is an issue which needs to be addressed by the industry and research bodies. In attempting an estimate of the current extent of the market, data from the BDO UK Hotel Industry reports has been analysed (see Appendix 1) to give a notional estimate of changes in the order of magnitude of the business. This is in no way to be taken as the genuine extent, merely as an indication of change. Using this data, which suggested a 9.73 per cent increase during the 1989–1995 period, it is estimated that by 1995 the market in Britain could have been worth £7.1 billion, representing 126.2 million delegate days. In terms of economic significance to the UK, the International Passenger Survey suggests that some £742 million is due to overseas business travellers attending UK conference, meeting and exhibition venues. As a generality, Elliott (1996) noted that every visitor to Britain spends an average of £500, and that every 'extra planeload adds seven extra jobs'. These figures give some indication, at least, of the importance both of business travel in general and also of conferencing in particular.

It is extremely difficult to quantify the concurrent figure for Ireland, due to a lack of reliable research data. However, the nature of the Irish economy, the importance of the role of tourism and the current extent of conference provision, together with the rural nature of much of Ireland and a limited number of large centres of population, might suggest a region comparable to that of the South West of England, and therefore a notional 9.5 million delegate days or a market worth somewhat about 500 million pounds to the Irish economy, and accounting for some, at least, of the 3.8 million visitors to Ireland (Nevin, 1995).

In the context of a community, the provision of a conference venue, be that venue purpose-built or be it a hotel or similar establishment, is often perceived as having a positive social and economic impact, in much the same way as the construction of a factory or tourist attraction would. The economic impact of hotels, (as conference venues) for example, on local communities is not as well documented (except in so far as local authorities are required to include hotel development analysis in their local structure planning) or researched as the large purpose-built venues. In the case of the latter, it is significant to bear in mind that the construction of purpose-built venues is often a matter of civic business, that is to say the development may be sponsored by the city or town council and based, partly at least, on the economic and social benefits that the development would bring to the community (Braun and Rungeling, 1992; Fenich, 1992). Given the size and extent of the conference market, economic and social benefits may be very great (Law, 1993). Figure 1.2 provides an example.

Clearly, this is development on a grand scale, but similar effects in terms of investment, employment, improvements to the environment and as a catalyst to other projects would be evident in the smaller civic-promoted conference centres around the country. This is not to say that such developments are without criticism; the *Birmingham Evening Mail* reported a £7.2 million loss on ICC operations in 1994, but noted that, taken as a whole, the ICC and its

In the case of the development of the International Convention Centre in Birmingham, it was felt that the Centre would result in:

- Provision of a 'world class' conference venue for the city.

- Regional investment of up to £40 million per annum.

- The security of up to 10 000 jobs indirectly, as well as the provision of 600 during the peak construction period and 2000 when linked to the city centre development.

- Related development of £1.6 billion.

- Complete redevelopment of the immediate area.

- The construction of two new hotels with a total of 464 rooms.

- 'Priming for an adjacent retail development.'

- Redevelopment and refurbishment of the area, in particular of a number of listed buildings and canalside projects.

Source: National Exhibition Centre Group, 1996; Law, 1993.

Figure 1.2 Economic benefits of conference centre development

associated venues were putting £438 million into the West Midlands economy, and since 1994 are making a profit.

1.4 Extent and scope of the conference business

The conference business is partly seasonal in nature, the peak period being September, October and November, the quietest period being the summer. This pattern of demand makes conferencing a particularly attractive activity in locations and establishments that rely, to a greater or lesser extent, on the summer tourist, as the two patterns of demand are complementary. In the earlier consideration of the economic and social benefits of conferencing, this seasonality throws into greater clarity the reasons why resort locations, in particular, have a considerable interest in developing their conference business (see Figure 1.3). Even in areas such as Cumbria, which have no major purpose-built centres, it is still possible to attempt to stimulate demand for conferences via promotional efforts by the Tourist Board or hotel consortia, geared to local hotels, as the conference business will help fill these hotels outside the peak tourist months.

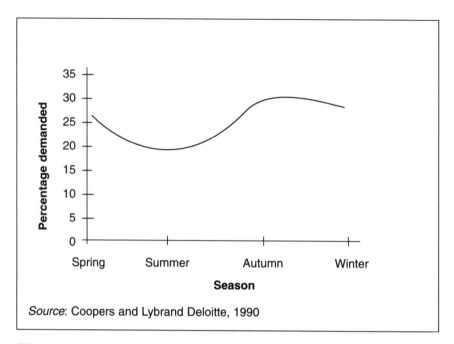

Figure 1.3   Seasonality of the conference business

Although the seasonality of the conference business has benefits in terms of its complementary nature to vacation tourism, a certain caution should be exercised in seeing conferences as a panacea in those areas where seasonal vacation tourism is relied upon. This is because the conference business is not spread equally in geographical terms. Demand is often driven by sectors which are mainly based in major urban areas. Even voluntary sector organizations may well have a head office, say in London, and regional offices in major centres such as Birmingham, Manchester or Newcastle. Similarly in Ireland, with a head office in Dublin, and regional offices in centres such as Cork, Galway, Sligo or Limerick.

Coopers and Lybrand Deloitte's survey indicated a very specific geographic bias in the spread of demand of delegate days. This spread, calculated alongside the 1995 forecast of delegate days would give a pattern as found in Table 1.1. In considering the geographic spread, a number of elements can be highlighted. The London area is the largest conference destination in the UK. Not only does London have a very large concentration of demand, including head offices of a significant number of organizations, it has also considerable demand from government bodies and from international organizations. The provision of conference venues is also a major contributor to London's strength: venues include the Queen Elizabeth II Conference Centre, the London Conference Forum, the Brewery Centre, the Cafe Royal, the Wembley Conference and Exhibition Centre etc.; London also has a high proportion of de luxe international hotels providing suitable conference and bedroom accommodation. The Midlands is also extremely significant as a conference destination. In particular, the International Convention Centre in Birmingham, the National Indoor Arena and the National Exhibition Centre, together with major venues in other Midland cities such as Sheffield, Leicester and Nottingham, and a high proportion of business hotels, would indicate the Midlands has every chance of becoming the foremost conference destination in the UK due to easier transport links, as opposed to the increasingly congested capital.

Table 1.1 Approximate delegate days in the UK conference market 1995

	Percentage of UK demand	*Notional delegate days*
London	35%	44.0 million
South East	10.5%	13.0 million
South West	7.5%	9.5 million
East Anglia	0.5%	0.6 million
Midlands	30%	38.0 million
North West	5%	6.0 million
North East	3%	3.8 million
Yorkshire	3%	3.8 million
Wales	2%	2.5 million
Scotland	2%	2.5 million
Northern Ireland	2%	2.5 million

Source: Author, based on Coopers and Lybrand Deloitte, 1990.

Of the remaining geographic spread, both the South East and parts of the South West benefit from satisfactory accessibility to London and to mainland Europe, particularly for the south coast resorts such as Brighton, Bournemouth and Torquay, which have large and well-established purpose-built centres with generally good hotel and travel infrastructure. East Anglia, conversely, while easily accessible from London, has no perceptible segment of the market and there are no large purpose-built centres anywhere in the East Anglian region; this, coupled with extremely poor intra-regional communications (except to Colchester and in the south of the region), serves to ensure that East Anglia is generally unattractive in terms of the overall conference destination pattern.

In the remainder of the UK, the pattern of demand for conference destinations is spread fairly equally, albeit with slight 'hot spots' in the North East and North West (including Manchester), though both these regions suffer somewhat from lack of adequate venues and sufficient hotel room provision. However, recent efforts by Manchester to reposition itself as a '24 hour' European city may result in development in conferencing and greater investment in facilities and hotels, some evidence of this being the opening of the GMEX Seminar Centre as an addition to the GMEX Exhibition Centre in Manchester in 1996.

It is not sufficient, however, to consider the UK and Ireland as relying on their own internal supply and demand factors. The International Passenger Survey has already noted a demand for conferencing of the order of 800 000 visitors to the UK alone per year. A large proportion of these are from the other parts of the (European) Union. A cause for concern for conference venues in both Britain and Ireland is that as communication networks improve (such as the Channel Tunnel and the proposals for de-regulation of air routes), there will be increased competition from venues in locations including Paris and Brussels. Therefore venues must seek to exploit the potential business to be had in the EU (worth some £90 billion – Coopers and Lybrand Deloitte, 1990) and from other non-domestic markets.

Summary

The history and development of the conference business, in both Britain and Ireland, has been closely related to the expansion of trade and the need for the interchange of ideas. The conference business is, in the contemporary world, significant both in social and economic terms as a contributor to local, regional and national development, a factor highlighted by the construction of flagship conference centres such as the ICC in Birmingham. Nevertheless, some regions have a more mature conference demand than others, and better provision, in a very competitive environment.

References

BDO (1989 et seq.) *UK Hotel Industry*, London, BDO Consultants.

Bramah, E. (1972) *Tea and Coffee*, London, Hutchinson, pp. 41–52.

Braun, B.M. and Rungeling, B. (1992) The relative economic impact of convention and tourist visitors on a regional economy. *International Journal of Hospitality Management*, 11(1), pp. 65–71.

Bruning, T. and Paulin, K. (1982) *Historic English Inns*, Newton Abbot, David and Charles, pp. 13–70.

Burkart, A.J. and Medlik, S. (1981) *Tourism: Past, Present and Future*, London, Heinemann, pp. 3–37.

Clout, H. (1991) *The Times London History Atlas*, London, Harper Collins, pp. 62–63.

Coopers and Lybrand (1990) *UK Conference Market Survey 1990*, London, Coopers and Deloitte Lybrand Deloitte Tourism and Leisure Consultancy Services, pp. 1–22.

Doran, S., Greenwood, M. and Hawkins, H. (1992) *Ireland: The Rough Guide*, London, Harrap – Columbus, pp. 529–542, 549–551.

Ellingham, M. (1994) *England: The Rough Guide*, London, Penguin, pp. 601–622.

Elliott, H. (1996) Britons say no to holidays at home. *The Times*, 3 October, p. 34.

Elliot, H. (1996) Britain is swinging again for young tourists. *The Times*, 3 October, p. 41.

Fenich, G.G (1992) Convention Centre Development: Pros, Cons and unanswered questions. *International Journal of Hospitality Management*, 11(3), pp. 183–196.

Girouard, M. (1990) *The English Town*, New Haven USA, Yale University Press, pp. 127–144, 289–313.

Greene, M. (1988) The Development of Management Techniques. In *Tourism a portrait*, (Horwath and Horwarth, eds), London, Horwath and Horwarth, pp. 21–26.

Law, C.M. (1993) *Urban Tourism*, London, Mansell, p. 39.

Loftman, P. and Nevin, B. (1992) *Urban regeneration and social equity, a case study of Birmingham 1986–1992*, Birmingham, University of Central England, Faculty of the Built Environment, Research Paper 38.

Morris, J. (1995) *The Age of Arthur*, London, Phoenix, (a) pp. 136–141, (b) pp. 151–163.

Murray, M. (1995) When will the balloon burst for convention centres? *Hospitality*, February/March, pp. 16–18.

National Exhibition Centre Group (1996) *Information Pack for the*

International Conference Centre. Birmingham, Birmingham, NEC Ltd (Unpublished), pp. 1–8.

Nevin, M. (1995) A case study in policy success: the development of the Irish tourism industry since 1985. *Journal of Vacation Marketing,* 13 March, pp. 363–375.

Shaw, G. and Williams, A. (1997) *The Rise and Fall of British Coastal Resorts,* London, Mansell, pp. 65–69.

Sunday Business (1996) Booming Overseas Visitors invest £742 million in U.K. Conference and Exhibition Industry. Editorial, *Sunday Business Newspaper,* London, 1 December, p. 31.

Taylor, D. (1977) *Fortune, Fame and Folly,* London, IPC, pp. 1–14.

2
The conference business and its market demand

The aims of this chapter are

1 To define the term 'conference' and consider the reasons why conferences take place.
2 To identify and classify the major demand generators for the conference business, into two principal categories: Corporate and Association.
3 To consider the corporate market in terms of its principal components together with the organizational aspects of the conference booking process for corporate businesses.
4 To consider the association market in terms of its principal components together with organizational aspects of the conference booking process for associations.
5 To categorize meetings in terms of the type of meeting or event being held.

2.1   Introduction

In identifying and analysing markets it is common to segment the whole. This categorization enables a closer examination of the component parts of the market. The demand generators for the conference business can be most conveniently categorized into the corporate market and the association market, or, roughly, profit-making and non-profit-making organizations. Later, it will be possible to see the importance of this categorization as an issue of targeting, by venue managements, of particular segments of these respective categories. In some respects the categorization is rather unusual compared to the way in which we might, for example, segment the market for hotels. With this latter it is often possible to identify individuals and classify according to age, reading patterns, social outlook and so on, thus enabling very specific sales or advertising tools to be used. With the conference business, we are dealing at an organizational level rather than an individual level. This organizational level has a number of implications for the use of sales or advertising tools and the approach of conference sales teams promoting their venues.

The corporate market tends to receive far more attention from venue managers than the association market. This is almost certainly due to a perceived relatively high average spend and perceived greater likelihood of repeat business. It is also likely that conference venues are more able to assess their chief potential corporate clients within a particular catchment area than is the case with the association market, some of which is voluntary and in which organizations' volunteer organizers may be extremely transient. There is also an evident difference of approach, for corporate clients rely increasingly on both internal and external agents to organize their conferences, and have the funding to do so, as well as pay for their own delegates (i.e. company employees) to attend. On the other hand the association client is more likely to be a volunteer with little or no experience of conference organization and needing greater levels of assistance from the venue.

2.2   What is a conference and why is it needed?

The Meetings Industry Association (1996) defines a conference as 'An event involving 10 or more people for a minimum of four hours during one day or more, frequently held outside the company's (sic) own premises'. However, this definition is rather prescriptive. Figure 2.1 illustrates the wider range of purposes for which conferences meet. There are also the more generalized functions of a conference, such as providing a vehicle to network with colleagues and, perhaps, as a vehicle to explore hidden agendas. Montgomery and Strick (1995), highlighting this, also make the point that corporations and associations have slightly differing needs for meetings: corporations may require meetings to disseminate information, plan, solve problems and train people; associations may require meetings more primarily for networking, education of members, planning and problem solving, and also to generate revenue.

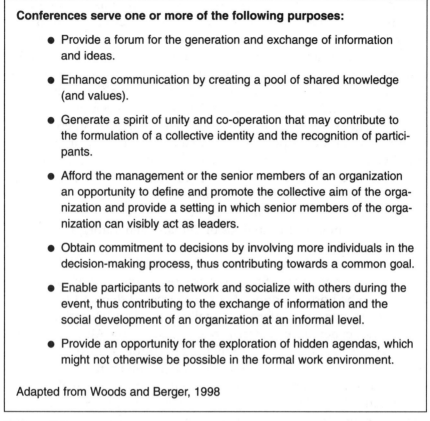

Conferences serve one or more of the following purposes:

- Provide a forum for the generation and exchange of information and ideas.

- Enhance communication by creating a pool of shared knowledge (and values).

- Generate a spirit of unity and co-operation that may contribute to the formulation of a collective identity and the recognition of participants.

- Afford the management or the senior members of an organization an opportunity to define and promote the collective aim of the organization and provide a setting in which senior members of the organization can visibly act as leaders.

- Obtain commitment to decisions by involving more individuals in the decision-making process, thus contributing towards a common goal.

- Enable participants to network and socialize with others during the event, thus contributing to the exchange of information and the social development of an organization at an informal level.

- Provide an opportunity for the exploration of hidden agendas, which might not otherwise be possible in the formal work environment.

Adapted from Woods and Berger, 1998

Figure 2.1

Conferences normally, but not exclusively, involve meeting in a given location with subsidiary activities such as the consumption of food and drink and the use of technical facilities. In both cases conference venues are exploiting one further need – the need to take staff or members out of their usual environment: where pressure of work may reduce the time available for meetings, where there may be constant interruptions or where the organization may simply not have the space to hold the meeting.

2.3 The identification of markets and demand generators

A great deal of conference activity is business related, but not exclusively so, as conferences involve not only commercial organizations, but also voluntary and non-corporate bodies. It is axiomatic of the conference business that the market can be classified into two general categories: first, corporate demand, secondly, association demand (Astroff and Abbey, 1985). In many surveys of the conference business, and in the view of a number of venue managers, it is the corporate market that is by far the more significant; however, such a view tends to reflect the ability of the corporate market to spend a larger sum on the organization of a particular conference. To concentrate on the corporate market alone would present an unbalanced view of the way in which demand is generated by various organizations. Indeed the Coopers and Lybrand Deloitte survey (1990) appears to make this very mistake, identifying sources of conference demand as being almost entirely corporate.

For the purpose of the analysis of demand generators, the classification into corporate and association demand will suffice, with the proviso that not all organizations, or all conference activities, will necessarily conveniently fit into these respective classifications. It should also be borne in mind that the sources of demand for a given conference centre or conference hotel in a particular location will be unlike the generalized pattern being discussed. Although some venues, such as the International Convention Centre (ICC) in Birmingham, may have a market catchment which ranges from the local to the international, a typical conference venue will be predominantly dependent on local sources of demand, be those local companies or other local organizations. The feasibility study of any new conference venue must therefore take great care to assess demand which is not only within a given catchment, but which could also be drawn away from competitor venues.

2.4   The corporate market

The corporate market is considered to be the largest demand generator in terms of income by the conference industry, though there is little research evidence at present to support the claim, merely the anecdotal views of venue managers. This is partly due to a lack of adequate analysis of demand and an inability to classify demand accurately. While venue managers are commonly able to say 'Company X is our largest corporate customer', it is rarer for venue managers also to be able to add 'forming X per cent of our total business'. The interpretation, used here, of corporate business is that the organization concerned should be profit making: public and private companies; the locally based small business, whether publicly or privately owned; and similar organizations.

The corporate market varies in its propensity to use conference venues, as certain types of organizations require the exchange of information (for management, sales, training or research) more frequently than others. Only the European Incentive Travel Survey (Touche Ross, 1990) attempted to classify key generators in the corporate sector; it nevertheless gives the only research overview of such demand. Respondents to that survey are shown by industry sector in Table 2.1. Such data must, however, be taken with a pinch of salt. Each conference venue could analyse not only its own existing business base, but also the industry composition of its own town, city or region, to highlight areas of demand. Analyses of this type would paint a far more accurate picture of a location's corporate demand than do the above figures. There is also a related issue of 'catchment area'. The Coopers and Lybrand Deloitte survey indicates that location is of serious importance to demand generators (or put more simply, conference organizers). About 70 per cent of organizers felt that a venue needed to be close to a motorway, but also, significantly, 50 per cent of organizers felt that venues needed to be both within one hour of a major city and within one hour of a major airport. These comments help to delineate the boundaries of the catchment of a conference venue and help to explain why regions such as East Anglia, with relatively poor transport networks and

Table 2.1   Corporate market demand – industry respondents

Pharmaceuticals	10%
Financial and insurance	10%
Cars	10%
Automotive parts	9%
Computing	9%
Toiletries/Cosmetics	9%
Electronics	9%
Electrical appliances	7%
Office equipment	6%
Agricultural equipment	5%
Retailers	5%
Building materials	5%
Heating/Air conditioning	4%
Leisure/Catering	1%
All others	2%

Source: Touche Ross (EITS 1990)

relatively poor provision, may fail to attract significant conference business.

A further aspect in assessing the corporate market is the issue of who would typically book a conference for an organization. This is a more significant question for the corporate market than the association market for reasons which will be explained later. Up until ten years ago, in the UK, the majority of corporate conferences were organized internally, by a manager or secretary within the organization. However, the downsizing of companies has seen a greater need to contract out activities, of which conference organization is one. Currently about half the corporate market is probably dealt with in-company (Coopers and Lybrand Deloitte, 1990), either directly by the company management or its support staff, or by a servicing department doing it on behalf of another division of the company. It is significant for the conference venue to know who, within the company requiring the conference, holds the budget for it. Of the remainder, conference placement agents account for about a quarter of corporate bookings. Quite simply, placement agents operate in very much the same way as any other agency activity; for a suitable commission they will make the link between venue and corporate client without the client having to become unduly involved in venue choice and arrangements.

In addition there are various types of 'middlemen'. There are, for example, an increasing number of conference production companies; such companies are particularly important where an organization requires highly technical or specialist services. A product launch would be a good example, there being a need for relatively complex visual and operational backup, above and beyond that required for, say, a basic training conference. Incentive travel companies are also involved in the conference business and fulfil an agency-type role where an organization needs to arrange not only a conference, say of its chief executives, but also some elements of travel, entertainment or perks required as a reward for good service or a prize-winning effort of staff within an organization.

A further aspect of the commercial market is the conference management companies which have a specific role in providing a service out of which they generate not a commission, but a profit. Typical examples are those companies providing training seminars in such subjects as information technology, human resources management, financial issues or sales training. These companies sell places at seminars or conferences to a wide range of organizations which may be too small or whose needs are too diverse for them to provide these services themselves. Companies of this kind, providing 'walk in' type conferences, meetings and seminars, will use a range of venues ranging from de luxe hotels to educational establishments, depending on the type of delegate and subject.

The corporate market has a known pattern of demand for the length of conferences. This pattern of demand has been identified in a number of surveys, including that reported by Richards (1996) for the English Tourist Board and shown in Figure 2.2.

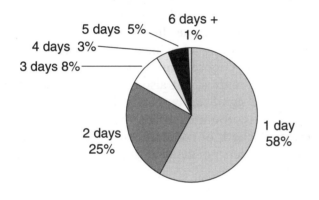

Source: Richards, 1996

Figure 2.2   Length of conference in the corporate market

2.5   The association market

Unlike the corporate market, the association market has received virtually no research attention and is, therefore, almost impossible to quantify, even anecdotally. Nevertheless the association market is extremely significant, and also extremely diverse. The interpretation used here of association business is that the organizations concerned are likely to be (though not exclusively) non-profit making. This interpretation allows us to take in an extremely wide range of organizations, some of which are run by salaried staff, some of which are run entirely by unpaid volunteers, and some of which may be governmental or quasi-governmental. The diversity of the association market is one reason why it is difficult to classify; a further reason is the concentration of venue managers on the corporate market, which is perceived, to a certain extent possibly wrongly, to be more profitable for venues. Nevertheless, the association market can be broadly split into professional associations on the one hand, and voluntary associations on the other.

The association market varies in its propensity to use conference venues as much as the corporate market, and for much the same reasons: a variety of organizational needs, differing management requirements and the extent to which information needs to be exchanged. Crucially, however, many of the organizations involved in the association market do not fund their own conference activity, but must charge their delegates the direct costs of doing so. This ensures that the association market is likely to be more price sensitive, having a propensity to choose venues such as educational establishments and municipal centres, but also that price sensitivity may determine location more significantly than is the case with the business market. As with the corporate market, there is a known pattern of demand in terms of length of conferences, which can be seen in Figure 2.3. There has been no detailed survey of the association

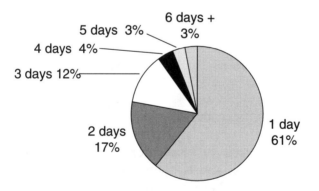

Source: Richards, 1996

Figure 2.3   Length of conference in the association market

market structure; consequently it is impossible to rank the importance of the various component organizations in any realistic way. Nevertheless the range of component organizations is significant and deserves elaboration.

Professional associations

This division includes trade, professional, scientific and technical associations, also national public associations, military associations and industrial bodies. Professional associations also comprise:

- **Government and agencies** This category includes national government bodies, local government bodies, chambers of commerce and agencies such as English Heritage and so on.
- **Trade unions and political parties** This category, self-evidently, contains not only all the political parties but also the TUC and its member unions.

Voluntary associations

This division includes organizations such as rotary clubs, the Lions, alumni societies, school groups and Womens' Institutes. Voluntary associations also comprise special interest groups such as sports clubs, hobby and craft clubs, lobbying groups, pressure groups and any organization with a closely defined purpose (e.g. a gardener's club):

- **Youth groups** This category includes youth clubs, organizations such as the YMCA or the Youth Hostelling Association, scouts and guides.
- **Voluntary and charitable bodies** A wide range of organizations ranging from charities such as 'Save the Children' to bodies such as the National Trust.
- **Religious groups** Including a wide variety of religious denominations and interest groups, church bodies and organizations such as the Salvation Army.

In much the same way as a conference venue could assess the corporate market in its catchment area, the same could be done for the association market. However, the process is rather more problematic. While the extent of the corporate business market may be obvious from such publications as a city or chamber of commerce guide, or an astute survey of the *Yellow Pages*, identification of the association market within a given catchment is limited because of the diversity and ad hoc nature of the organizations involved. Indeed many of the organizations within the voluntary association market may not even have a public phone number, central office or secretary. Assessment of this market will require a careful analysis of past data, monitoring of competitors' business and assiduous record keeping about the local community.

The organization of conferences for the association market relies much less on agencies and production companies, and a great deal more on the efforts of often unpaid volunteers. This poses a challenge for venue managers and sales teams, not only in identifying who, in an association, is likely to be the conference organizer, but also in terms of dealing with organizers who lack the necessary experience and skills. In consequence sales teams may have to exert greater efforts to ensure an association conference goes smoothly than might be the case when dealing with a more experienced placement agent or a contact within a commercial organization whose specific duties include conference organization.

2.6   Types of conference

In addition to categorizing, or segmenting, demand generators, it is also possible to consider the conference business in terms of the purpose for which the conference is being organized. The most common range of purposes are summarized in Figure 2.4, and include the following.

Small executive meetings
This type of conference, in which the number of delegates is usually less than 20, is the largest single category. It is a type which is particularly suited to hotel conference venues, and is especially important to the country house hotel sector. These meetings are usually fulfilling a managerial, planning or problem solving role.

Training events
This type of conference normally varies in size from the more common smaller event, again with fewer than 20 people, to some

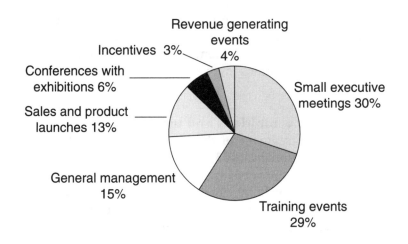

Source: Coopers and Lybrand Deloitte, 1990

Figure 2.4   Segmentation by type of conference

quite large 'educational' training events of up to 200 people. The events are again suited to the hotel sector, though with a tendency to concentrate more on city or regional locations (or those associated with company head offices, divisional offices, and management training centres).

General management
This type of conference, including everything from routine management to Annual General Meetings, has expanded significantly due to the increase in company restructuring taking place and the need to discuss and inform an organization about changes in management or policy. Meetings normally range from the small to the relatively large – 300 or so is a common figure. While hotel conference venues are important, the larger events in this category begin to use purpose-built venues.

Sales and product launches
This type of event probably involves not only a conference but also an exhibition as the raison d'être of the event. Such launches are generally large affairs and require not only extensive organizational effort but also significant technical facilities. Events of this type are

most common in purpose-built venues. Indeed there is some evidence to indicate a shortage of the largest type of venues for these events (Law, 1993). In terms of the sales conference (or exhibition involving a corporate dealership), large venues are required and also probably some element of incentive, thus dealership conferences and exhibitions may take place in more specialist or unique venues.

Conferences with exhibitions and trade fairs
An extremely large segment of the business, estimated to have an exhibition expenditure, in 1993, of some £740 million (Keynote, 1994), ranging from the very small, such as an art show, to the very large such as a boat or home show. Purpose-built venues are often used, though hotels and a wide range of other venues are also able to provide suitable space and adjacent conference facilities.

Incentive conferences
While it can be argued that most conferences have the incentive of 'uniqueness' away from the daily routine of commercial or organizational life, there is a demand for conferences which have an overt incentive package, involving some aspects of travel/tourism or special event as part of the conference. The Touché-Ross European Incentive Travel Survey 1990 looked at this business in some detail and concluded that it was a particularly lucrative part of the market, tending to use both de luxe hotel venues and also unique venues as part of the package.

Revenue generation events
Both for associations and for conference management companies, revenue generation is a significant part of organizing a conference. Events of this kind are often educational or informative but contribute to the organizer's financial viability. Conferences or meetings of this kind are often held in universities or colleges or small hotel locations to keep costs down.

Summary

Conferences, large and small, exist as a means of exchanging information and as a forum for many related inter-social activities. There are many sources of demand for conferences, but we have, for convenience, categorized them in two ways: first, by market origin into corporate and association markets, then into various subdivisions; secondly, by the type of conference itself.

References

Astroff, M.T. and Abbey, J.R. (1985) *Convention Sales and Services*, New Jersey, Waterbury Press, pp. 69–110.

Coopers and Lybrand Deloitte (1990) *UK Conference Market Survey 1990*, London, Coopers and Lybrand Deloitte Tourism and Leisure Consultancy Services, pp. 7–13.

Cotterell, P. (1994) *Conferences: An Organizer's Guide*, Sevenoaks, Hodder and Stoughton, pp. 1–12.

Keynote Reports (1994) *Keynote Report, A Market Sector Overview: Exhibitions & Conferences*, London, Keynote Publications, pp. 29–32.

Law, C.M. (1993) *Urban Tourism*, London, Mansell, pp. 39–68.

Meetings Industry Association (1996) *UK Conference Market Survey 1996*, Broadway, Meetings Industry Association, pp. 1–32.

Montgomery, R.J. and Strick, S.K. (1995) *Meetings, Conventions and Expositions*, New York, Van Nostrand Reinhold, pp. 66–64.

Richards, B. (1996) The conference market in the UK. In *Insights*, London, English Tourist Board, pp. B-67–B-83.

Touche Ross (1990) *The European Incentive Travel Survey 1990*, London, Touche Ross, pp. 100–102.

Woods, R.H. and Berger, F. (1988) Making Meetings Work. *Cornell Hotel and Restaurant Quarterly*, **29**, pp. 101–105.

3

The provision and supply of conference venues

The aims of this chapter are:

1 To examine the range of conference venues and to highlight the different characteristics of each.
2 To explore and quantify the geographic spread of conference venues within Britain and Ireland in terms of a regional analysis and regional variations.
3 To examine the nature of the ownership and management of conference venues in the light of funding and organizational issues in general.

3.1   Introduction

In the first chapter we referred to the history and development of conference venues and the attempts by interested bodies, such as consultants and academics, to classify them. Some of these classifications do not adequately explain the characteristics of the various venue types. However, an exploration of characteristics is a necessary step in the exploration of the structure and components of the supply side of the conference business. For the benefit of students, current examples are given which may serve to assist understanding of the classification. There are elements of overlap between the classifications and it should be noted that the classification is intended as a 'modus vivendi' (or put more simply, the classification will develop as time goes on), not as the last word.

In addition to the classification, an analysis has been carried out of published information, notably the 'Conference Blue Book' to attempt to quantify the geographic spread of venues. Each (UK) region is identified with a percentage of venues as a proportion of the whole and, where possible, the number of large-scale venues are noted (large scale being defined as a centre capable of accommodating 1000 or more people) together with an identification of purpose-built conference centres in each region, where these are known.

Clearly there are limitations to this type of analysis as the published or advertised information about venues represents only a fraction of the actual total. Related to this constraint is the issue of 'when is a conference centre not a conference centre', given that, arguably, any room capable of taking two people round a table for a small fee could be classed as a conference venue.

Conference centres are not evenly spread throughout the country; this is partly a function of demand, partly a function of existing infrastructure and competition, and partly a function of the need or ability of a town, city or resort to develop conferencing as part of the economic provision of that place. Large conference centres provide employment and other economic benefits, but they are not the only means of doing this; in consequence, given limited funds, a council or other public or private body may decide that a conference centre may not be the only economic option possible in their location.

Conference centres, which, in general terms, can be seen as a homogeneous business activity, vary considerably in their development and original funding. The largest centres are often a product of combined public and private sector funding and play a role in the economic well-being of a city, town or resort area. Funding and origins do vary from sector to sector and as a consequence, each sector is taken individually. Essentially, funds for the development of a conference venue may be obtained on the open market, that is to say via banks and shareholder investment; or via public sources such as city councils, government (or the European Union), or national funds, including the lottery, sports and arts councils, depending on the type of development. In a very limited number of cases, a conference centre may be privately owned by a single individual or small group of individuals. Regardless of who owns the venue, we can see the proportion of the total market that different venues hold in Figure 3.1.

Whatever the ownership, management structure or proportion of the total business a conference venue has, the primary objective of its development is likely to be the generation of wealth. This depends on there being an adequate market for the centre's services (poor market feasibility analysis may result in a centre being opened where there is inadequate demand, resulting in bankruptcy and closure) and/or the

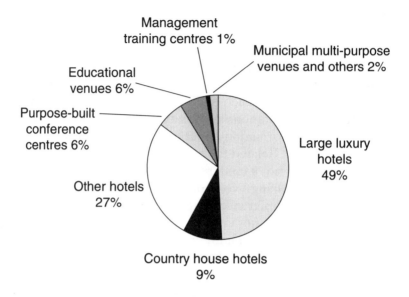

Source: Coopers and Lybrand Deloitte, 1990

Figure 3.1   Percentage share of delegate days by type of venue

effectiveness of the management of that centre. As with hotels, the management of a centre may make all the difference to its profitability (Lundberg, 1994) but as centres have high capital costs, so the market demand and general state of the economy are also important.

3.2   The range of conference venues and their ownership and management

Fundamental to any examination of the issues of ownership and management of conference venues is an understanding of the differences between ownership, on the one hand, and management on the other. While the difference is generally clear to the experienced observer, it is often less so to the student. In former days, and for small organizations, the 'ownership' and 'management' were often the same. The person who ran a small inn with a meeting room, in a country town, both owned the property and managed the business, many still do. The larger the business, and many conference venues are very large businesses indeed, the more likely and necessary the separation of ownership and management becomes. It should also be considered that a particular venue may not fall conveniently into a particular class. The major classes are, for our analysis, as follows.

Purpose-built conference centres

These centres are the ones that probably spring to mind when the words 'conference centre' or 'convention centre' are used. In general, these venues are large, modern, high profile and constructed by a municipality or dedicated company with a view to profit or the economic benefit to the community (Fenich, 1995). Of these, there are a number which are particularly well known: the International Convention Centre (ICC) in Birmingham, the Harrogate International Centre and the Conference Forum in London are examples. The ICC includes Birmingham Symphony Hall, home of the City of Birmingham Symphony Orchestra. The Harrogate International Centre is one of a number of purpose-built centres constructed to rejuvenate resort or spa towns. The Conference Forum contains the Chaucer Theatre and was intended to contribute to the community life of the Aldgate area of the city of London. Such purpose-built centres are often, therefore, extremely significant to their areas, both in economic and social terms. They are thought of as the flagships of the conference business and there are fewer than 30 in the whole of the UK, and none in Ireland, whose principal business is conferencing. Owing to their purpose-built nature, they are generally technically advanced, have large auditoria and good support infrastructure such as parking and loading facilities.

Historically, purpose-built conference centres were often developed out of some civic initiative (i.e. by a local or regional council). They were often intended to play a role in maintaining a town's economic future, so some of the older purpose-built conference centres were developed and owned by the councils themselves, particularly in resort towns. As demand for larger-scale venues increased, however, civic funds were limited and town councils were no longer in a position to develop centres from their own funds. Various partnership arrangements were created in order to build and operate conference centres, where centres were needed for a public purpose, such as economic development or regeneration, but money came from other sources, mainly the commercial sector, with possible input from the European Union or the National Lottery. The International Convention Centre and National Indoor Arena (NIA) in Birmingham can be used to illustrate this type of ownership. Both land and buildings are owned by Birmingham City Council, but are operated by a management company, NEC Ltd, the share capital of which is owned equally by the City Council and the Birmingham

Chamber of Commerce. The capital funding of the ICC was composed of a loan stock issue of £130 million via NEC Ltd and a further £50 million grant from the European Regional Development Fund (EU). In contrast, the NIA capital funding was comprised of £22 million from the city council, £3 million from the UK Sports Council and a private development company (Shearwater) providing £25 million (Law, 1993; NEC, 1996).

Municipal multi-purpose centres

The construction or development of a purpose-built conference centre is hugely expensive. As a consequence, the cost, even taking into account large private sector funding, is beyond the ability of most municipalities (towns) to promote, or indeed to justify in terms of demand. It is therefore often the case that a town or city will construct a multi-purpose facility or reuse a former civic building as a conference venue. There are a number of excellent examples of such multi-use: the Dome in Doncaster provides conferencing, leisure facilities, sports facilities and a wide range of subsidiary activities. It is a new purpose-designed venue, of a type (or approach) found in other locations such as the Plymouth Pavilions or the Aviemore Mountain Resort. A less costly approach to the type of venue is that adopted by locations such as Eastbourne, whose Devonshire Park Centre comprises a historic Winter Garden and the Congress Theatre; or the Albert Halls in Bolton, developed from a former hall of the formidable Victorian stature and civic pride so often found in the towns and cities of Northern England and Northern Ireland. Venues of this type are often of a high standard, but occasionally limitations in the public purse (council funds) result in a lack of investment, implying that some multi-purpose centres may not exploit their full potential.

The ownership and management of this class of venues are similar, in some respects, to those of the purpose-built conference centres. They are largely funded by councils, but increasingly with some of the money provided by private sources, including developers, and, in a few cases, by the National Lottery or European Union. Management, as a generality, is of two kinds: in-house (i.e. managed as a department of the council) or via a management company set up by the council and its partners. In a few cases, these centres may be run by an operating company on a contractual basis, e.g. a facilities management company with interests in the leisure/hospitality or arts field. The Dome at Doncaster is probably the largest example in the UK. It was opened in 1989 at a cost of £25 million, and funded by Doncaster Metropolitan Borough Council. It provides not only conference facilities but also extensive leisure pools, split-level ice rink, a beauty therapy suite, fitness facilities, a bowls hall, a 2000-seater events hall and a forum area for exhibitions and special events. It is estimated that the Dome has also attracted some £20 million of additional inward investment to the immediate area. The Dome is run by a private limited company together with a group of trustees from the council and community who oversee general policy (Dome, 1994).

Residential conference centres and in-company facilities

A number of this type of centre exist; they are, if not purpose-built, at least purposely converted, often from buildings of some architectural distinction. Most are operated by private companies, whose raison d'être is management development or conference centre provision as a commercial activity. The standard of the upper echelon of such centres is extremely high; there are, however, a number of centres whose raison d'être is more management development in an activity sense, i.e. not entirely classroom based but involving outdoor activities of various kinds. Examples of the former are the Sundridge Park Management Centre in Bromley and the Ashridge Management College in Berkhamsted. Examples of the latter are often found in National Parks, sometimes run by the Park Authority and having a purpose of, primarily, outdoor education; in these cases the facilities may be extremely basic and deliberately so due to the nature of their main function of outdoor education, or team building.

Similar in concept to many residential conference centres (though not always with residential accommodation), a large number of companies have their own in-company conference centres. These may range from relatively small on-premises facilities to large out of town venues, particularly for large national organizations such as banks, building societies and insurance companies (e.g. the BBC's Wood Norton Conference Centre in Evesham and the Siemens Company Conference Centre in Manchester). These companies have a constant need for staff training and conferencing for whom full-scale in-company facilities prove more cost-effective than external venues.

Both these types of centres tend to be wholly owned and managed by the companies themselves, with a few being managed by operating companies. Residential conference centres may be very similar in ownership and management to the hotel sector. Hayley Conference Centres, for example, owning several residential conference centres in the South Midlands, bear a number of similarities to hotel-owning companies. In-company facilities, such as those used by the major banks or insurance companies for staff training purposes, are, in a few cases, operated by the companies themselves, but increasingly the operations and management are contracted out to an operator, typically one of the major contract catering companies such as Sutcliff, Aramark or Town and County.

Academic venues

A large number of universities and colleges provide conference facilities; this is particularly the case where such institutions seek to generate income during vacation periods, when their extensive provision of lecture theatres, technical facilities and residential accommodation is available for external use. In practice, summer conferencing is particularly important for many academic institutions and indeed a number of them provide not only summer use facilities but also dedicated conferencing facilities all year round. Examples include the Penthouse Conference Centre of the University of Durham, UMIST's Manchester Conference Centre at Weston Hall and the Danbury Park Management Centre of Anglia University at Chelmsford. The list of universities and colleges offering conferencing is very long indeed. Academic venues are also, significantly, of considerable importance to the association market, due to cost competitiveness. While some academic venues offer extremely high quality conferencing and many, such as the University of Surrey and UMIST, are able to provide bedroom accommodation to an en-suite standard, many only provide student 'study bedroom' accommodation sharing communal facilities between conference delegates, one reason for the relatively modest cost.

Almost all academic venues are owned and managed in-house; this is chiefly due to them being used principally for educational purposes during the academic year, rather than as conference venues, year round. Most universities and colleges seriously involved in the business have a separate (though still in-house) conference office to deal with the business, though many rely on the provision of the services within the conference areas being dealt with by outsourced companies (e.g. contract caterers or facility management organizations). Conferences are, however, a major source of income to most universities and colleges; as a consequence, some of these have developed their conference business significantly and have sought external funding for the building of residential facilities and to improve the quality of their conference areas. Historically, academic venues sought to use their lecture rooms and halls of residence during vacation periods for the conference business, and this continues. On the other hand, an increasing number have sought some private sector funding to construct either complete year-round residential conference venues (such as UMIST's Manchester Conference Centre) or to construct higher quality residential facilities with en-suite rooms for conference delegates (such as at the University of Surrey, University of Essex and elsewhere).

Hotels

The importance of hotels to the conference business must not be underestimated. Hotels are the largest single component classification of venue providers, with in excess of 70 per cent of the provision (Coopers and Lybrand Deloitte, 1990). Owing to this strength of provision, and the varying nature of hotels themselves, this class is sub-categorized into three: de luxe city centre hotels; country house hotels; other hotels.

De luxe city centre hotels
To say 'city centre' is rather a misnomer, as we are really talking of any urban conurbation, some towns, some cities. The de luxe element is crucial and is chiefly in those establishments that the public would think of as four or five star rated. The range and diversity, even within the sub-classification, are considerable and the extent of the provision renders examples unnecessary – just pick up any hotel guide.

Country house hotels
As with the above, country house hotels are extremely diverse but, as a generality, are of a very high standard and are often located in their own grounds. The major development of country house hotels in recent years has been by conversion of former stately homes, some of which are both extremely historical and stupendously grand, some of which are more modest, but delighting in their rural setting. As with city centre hotels, the list is extremely long.

Other hotels

It is rather unfair to class all other hotels this way, but the sub-classifications could run into a very extensive list indeed, ranging from ancient inns, Georgian town house hotels and Victorian railway hotels to modern airport hotels – from the chain lodge to the family-run establishment. A very large number of hotels provide conference facilities, ranging from a single room to whole conference wings attached to large hotels. In particular, a number of the major hotel companies, such as Stakis and Mount Charlotte Thistle in Britain, and Jury's in Ireland, concentrate on providing conference and leisure facilities in their business hotels.

It has been noted that the largest provider of conference venues is the hotel sector. Ownership of hotels runs from private individuals to major international public companies, whose shareholders own the business. In between these extremes are partnerships and private companies (large and small). Private companies have a limited number of owners, say a group of six people, for example, who have put money into the business. Public companies are those quoted on the stock market, whose ownership may be composed of a very large number of small shareholders or some large shareholders and shareholding institutions, such as pension funds. The activities of these various types of owning groups (companies) vary, even in the hotel sector. Some are purely hotel owning or operating companies such as Jarvis and Inter-Continental; some have hospitality businesses in related sectors, including restaurants and other service activities, such as Granada and Whitbread; some have major interests in non-hospitality businesses, such as Virgin, First Leisure and Ladbrokes. Clearly, ownership and management also vary, even within this apparently unified sector. Companies with hotels (and therefore conference interests) may both own the property and manage it; alternatively, they may not own the property, but own the brand name and act as operators by contract to the property owners; or finally, they may own the property but have another organization manage it by operating contract, franchise, leaseback or other specialist contractual arrangement.

Unusual venues

The final class is in fact 'everything else'. This is not as simple as it seems. It includes any place with a room able to accommodate two or more people around a table for a meeting which either cannot be categorized anywhere else and/or has some unique feature as shown in Figure 3.2. The extent of the 'unusual venue' category is enormous. The demand by conference organizers and particularly from incentive travel organizers for a venue which is unique, whether that uniqueness is in a castle or a cave is extremely significant. Many venues of this kind also tend to be at the upper end of the price range.

- Ships – Car ferries to battleships

- Castles and country houses/stately homes – Warwick Castle to Castle Howard

- Sports venues – Race courses to dog tracks

- Gardens – Botanical gardens to Winter gardens

- Museums – Motorcycle museums to Madame Tussauds

- Entertainment – Coronation Street to Whipsnade Wild Animal Park

- Listed buildings – The Royal Pavilion, Brighton to the Old Palace, Hatfield

- Institutes – Chartered Accountants to the Royal Society of Art

- Theatres – Royal National Theatre, London to the Crucible, Sheffield

---

Figure 3.2 Examples of unique venues

The ownership and management of unusual venues are as varied as the class itself. However, it does contain a proportion of organizations not found in the other categories – charities. Whereas the majority of conference venues are owned and managed by commercial or quasi-commercial organizations, many unusual venues, particularly in the castles/listed buildings and museums categories, are owned and operated by charities and similar organizations such as, in the UK, the National Trust, National Parks authorities, heritage organizations and voluntary bodies, and comparable Irish organizations, including private individuals. Clearly, a number of charities do have specific commercial aims and departments responsible for revenue generation through retailing, catering or conferencing. Funding of refurbishment or new construction in this field is therefore from charitable income, investments or possibly in the UK, through bids to the National Lottery, Millennium Fund, Arts or Sports Councils and in Ireland, the Lotto or heritage agencies and similar bodies, with advice from regional tourism organizations.

3.3   Geographic spread of venues

It is probably impossible ever to count the total number of conference venues in Britain and Ireland. The reasons are similar in some respects to those true of the hotel industry – picking up any hotel guide may give the reader a view of the comparative order of magnitude of provision in one area versus another, but a simple comparison of the listing of a particular town in, say, the *AA Guide* and the *Yellow Pages* telephone directory of that town would prove the difference: a typical hotel guide will list only a small proportion of the total because many guides are a form of paid advertising, whereas the telephone directory should list every hotel, inn and guest house in a town. This comparison cannot easily be made for conference venues – the telephone directory does not list them in the comprehensive way that hotels are listed. The estimation of size and extent of conference venues as an industry can only be guessed at, but a comparison of the order of magnitude of provision in different areas can be achieved. The analysis here is based on data provided in the *Conference Blue Book 1996* and from data supplied by the Convention Bureau of Ireland. The *Blue Book* guide lists approximately 4450 conference venues in the UK and a comparison, region by region, is possible.

3.4   Regional variations in provision

The South West of England (Figure 3.4)
Including Cornwall, Devon, Somerset, Dorset, City and County of Bristol, North Somerset, Bath and North East Somerset, Wiltshire, Hampshire, the Isle of Wight and the Channel Islands; 14 per cent of total venues, with 31 venues capable of accommodating over 1000 people (theatre style). Purpose-built venues include the Bournemouth International Centre and the Torquay Riviera Centre.

The South East of England (Figure 3.5)
Including Surrey, Kent, East and West Sussex (Brighton and Hove); 8 per cent of total venues, with 13 venues capable of accommodating over 1000 people. Purpose-built venues include the Brighton Centre.

Greater London (Figure 3.6)
Including the cities of London and Westminster and the London boroughs; 8.5 per cent of total venues, with 27 venues capable of accommodating over 1000 people. However, a number of these large venues

Figure 3.3 Orientation of Britain and Ireland. Figures 3.3–13 identify county boundaries, county towns (if known) and locations identified in the text

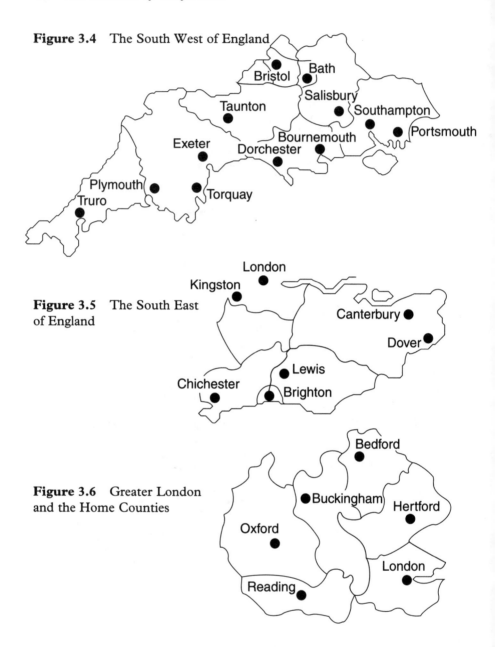

Figure 3.4   The South West of England

Figure 3.5   The South East of England

Figure 3.6   Greater London and the Home Counties

are London theatres and thus the availability of space at appropriate times could be subject to restrictions due to performances. Purpose-built venues include the Queen Elizabeth II Conference Centre, the Conference Forum, Wembley Conference and Exhibition Centre, the London Arena and the Barbican Centre.

The Home Counties of England (Figure 3.6)
Including Hertfordshire, Bedfordshire, Buckinghamshire, Oxford-shire and Berkshire; 7 per cent of total venues, with five venues capable of accommodating over 1000 people. There are no major purpose-built centres in this region, and for convenience the Home Counties were included as part of the 'Midlands' in the earlier section on regional demand.

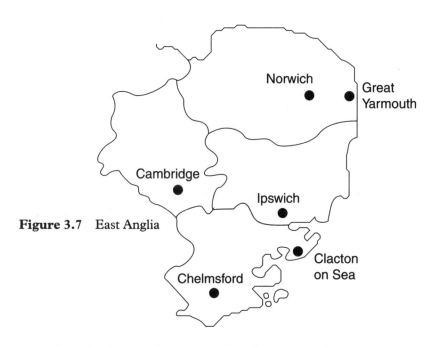

Figure 3.7   East Anglia

The East Anglia region of England (Figure 3.7)
Including Essex, Cambridgeshire, Suffolk, Norfolk; 5.5 per cent of total venues, with nine venues capable of accommodating over 1000 people (of which four, by some curious circumstance, are in Great Yarmouth). There are no purpose-built venues here.

The English Midlands (Figure 3.8)
Including Lincolnshire, North Lincolnshire and North East Lincolnshire, Nottinghamshire, Derbyshire, Northamptonshire, Leicestershire, County of Rutland, Staffordshire, West Midlands Conurbation (Birmingham, Wolverhampton etc.), Shropshire, Warwickshire, County of Hereford and Worcester, Gloucestershire; 15 per cent of total venues, with 34 venues capable of accommodating over 1000 people. Purpose-built venues: the International Convention Centre, National Exhibition Centre, National Indoor Arena.

Figure 3.8   The English Midlands

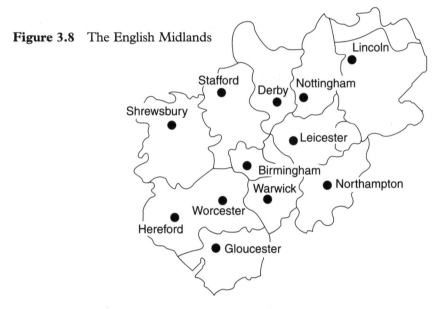

The North West of England (Figure 3.9)
Including Cumbria, County Palatine of Lancashire, Manchester, Merseyside, Cheshire; 11 per cent of total venues, with 30 venues capable of accommodating over 1000 people. Purpose-built venues include the GMEX Seminar Centre and the Bridgewater Hall, Manchester. Large-scale centres also include Blackpool Winter Gardens.

Figure 3.9   The North West of England

The North East of England and Yorkshire (Figure 3.10)
Including Northumberland, Redcar and Cleveland, Stockton-on-Tees, Middlesbrough, Darlington, Hartlepool, Tyne and Wear, County of Durham, City of Kingston-upon-Hull, City of York, North Yorkshire, South Yorkshire, West Yorkshire and the East Riding of Yorkshire; 13 per cent of total venues, with 30 venues capable of accommodating over 1000 people. Purpose-built venues include the Harrogate International Centre and Conference 21 Sheffield.

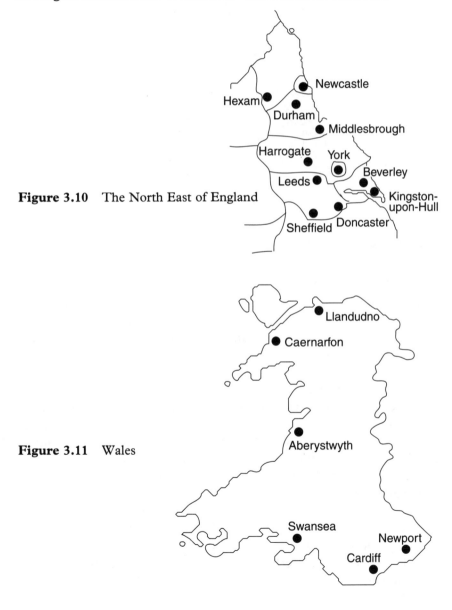

Figure 3.10   The North East of England

Figure 3.11   Wales

Figure 3.12   Scotland

Wales (Figure 3.11)
Wales has 4.5 per cent of total venues, with nine venues capable of accommodating over 1000 people. Purpose-built venues include the Cardiff International Arena and the North Wales Conference Centre, Llandudno.

Scotland (Figure 3.12)
Scotland has 11 per cent of total venues, with 24 venues capable of accommodating over 1000 people. Purpose-built venues include the Aberdeen Exhibition and Conference Centre, the Edinburgh Conference Centre, the Edinburgh International Conference Centre and the Scottish Exhibition and Conference Centre, Glasgow.
Northern Ireland (Figure 3.13)

Northern Ireland has 2 per cent of total venues, with six venues capable of accommodating over 1000 people. Purpose-built venues include the Belfast Waterfront Hall. The King's Hall is one of the major large-scale centres.

Ireland (Figure 3.13)
The proportion of venues in the foregoing analysis has excluded Ireland, but Figure 3.13 illustrates the major locations in the republic. Ireland has a number of venues capable of accommodating over 1000 people. In Dublin this includes the National Concert Hall, the Point Theatre, the Burlington Hotel, the Royal Dublin Society ('RDS') and University College, Dublin. Other large-scale venues can be found in Athlone, Bundoran, Cork, Ennis, Galway, Killarney, Letterkenny, Limerick, Tivoli, Tralee and Waterford.

Figure 3.13   Northern Ireland and Ireland

Summary

This chapter has considered the various types of conference venue to be found within the United Kingdom and Ireland. While we may typically think of conference centres as being large purpose-built operations, most are not; the largest single component sector is, in fact, hotels. Venues are available in a large geographic spread, but certain areas lend themselves to the provision of conference venues, typically due to their location and accessibility to the market; hence concentrations around London and Birmingham in the UK and Dublin in Ireland.

References

Coopers and Lybrand Deloitte (1990) *UK Conference Market Survey 1990*, London, Coopers and Lybrand Deloitte Tourism & Leisure Consultancy Service, pp. 1–22.

Dome (1994) *An adventure into the world of leisure*, Doncaster, Doncaster Leisure Management Ltd (unpublished).

Expotel (1993 *The Expotel and Conference Centre Insiders Guide to Conference Planning*, London, Expotel.

Fenich, G.G. (1995) Convention Centre Operations: Some questions answered. *International Journal of Hospitality Management*, 14(3/4), pp. 311–324.

Keynote (1994) *Key Note Report, a Market Sector Overview. Exhibitions and Conferences*, London, Keynote, pp. 5–9.

Law, C.M. (1993) *Urban Tourism*, London, Mansell, pp. 55–61.

Lundberg, D.E. (1994) *The Hotel and Restaurant Business*, New York, Van Nostrand Reinhold, pp. 72–89.

Miller Freeman (1996) *The Conference Blue Book 1996* (General Venues). Tonbridge, Miller Freeman Technical Ltd.

Miller Freeman (1996) *The Conference Green Book 1996* (Special Interest Venues). Tonbridge, Miller Freeman Technical Ltd.

Montgomery, R.S. and Strick, S.K. (1995) *Meetings, Conventions and Expositions*, New York, Van Nostrand Reinhold, pp. 9–15.

National Exhibition Centre, (1996) *Information Pack for the International Conference Centre. Birmingham*, Birmingham, NEC Ltd (Unpublished), pp. 1–8.

Savills Commercial (1994) *Property – Finance and Investment 5/95*, London, Savills Commercial Research, pp. 2–4.

4

Related services

The aims of this chapter are:

1 To provide an overview of the type of additional services available to conference organizers and venue managers.
2 To consider these services in the organizational context and the difference between services which may be said to be 'packaged' and those which are self-standing and the sole activity of one type of company in the field.

4.1 Introduction

The conference business is not solely concerned with the provision of meeting rooms, refreshment and technical equipment; it encompasses a wide range of related activities. Although the most basic type of conference may require only those things, the larger and more elaborate conferences become, the greater the need for increased technical support, thus conference organizers and conference venues can draw upon a sophisticated range of additional support services to ensure events go well.

Owing to the increasing complexity of hi-tech presentation methods and the standard of organization needed for complex conferences, product launches, and events such as roadshows, a whole series of specialist companies have grown up to service these needs. These companies, typically, either package services and provide the whole thing, or provide one element of the service needed by a conference organizer or venue manager who may wish to do the rest him/herself.

Companies which are capable of providing complete packages esentially fall into three categories:

Conference production companies
Exhibition contractors
Event management companies

All three are relatively common, though each has a slightly different orientation, i.e. conference presentation and staging; exhibition design; hospitality events of one kind or another.

In addition to these types of organizations, a wide range of companies provide support services which can be hired in, contracted or purchased (depending on the service). These cover both directly related services, such as the provision of accommodation and hospitality for delegates, and indirect services which exist not only to provide something for the conference business but also perform a function for the local community. These include: technical services in the presentation field, providing equipment, and sometimes training, for speakers; transport and guiding services, whose role is to get delegates from the point of arrival to, and sometimes around, a conference venue; and various other services such as translation, medical, crèche, administration, secretarial and business support (Kotas and Jayawardena, 1994).

The use of these various organizations is a matter not only of budget, but also of the experience (or lack of it) of conference organizers and venue management, of the standard to be achieved at a given conference, of the time available to make arrangements and of the requirements of the organization making the booking. Needs and, therefore, the approach, vary.

4.2   Conference production companies

Venue buyers and conference organizers are often confronted with unique problems when seeking to create conferences of a professional standard. This is particularly the case for high profile events. The ability to develop such events may be beyond the knowledge of the average conference organizer, delegated to do the job within a company or association. Nevertheless, high profile events, roadshows, major exhibitions and product launches all require specialist technical facilities and knowledge. Increasingly, events of this kind are put into the hands of conference production companies, which specialize in the creation of events to a high standard.

Production companies are able to package together the wide range of technical support that high profile conferences often require. This technical support ranges from set design to the training of presenters. A production company will probably be able to undertake most, or all, of the following activities:

- Project management, in the case of conferences where the whole event is delegated by the organizer to the production company;
- Design, including set and backdrop design, staging, lighting and all the range of audio visual support needed for high quality presentations;
- Venue management, where an organization may, for example, wish to take over a unique venue, such as a museum or National Trust property, to use for its conference and requires expertise to be brought in which the venue itself might not normally possess;
- Delegate handling, which ranges from the simplest issues of delegate check-in and registration to the full provision of accommodation booking and allocation of accommodation for delegates;
- Technical support, ranging from simple provision or hiring in of equipment to the full preparation of computer graphics, slide or video production and related facilities;
- Training of presenters, speakers and moderators, often including not only the basic training but also scriptwriting and autocue use.

Naturally, the packaging of the whole conference production process does not come cheaply, but production companies have a level of expertise that most conference organizers do not possess, so that while it would be possible for a conference organizer to put together a highly complex up-market conference, the organizer would have to be both well trained and extremely experienced to do so. Given that few organizations in either the corporate or association market possess full-time conference organizers, the need to bring in production companies for events of a high profile nature is clear.

4.3 Exhibition contractors

In addition to conference production companies, there are two other types of organizations which undertake related activities with much the same approach as a production company. These are exhibition contractors and event management companies (sometimes called 'ground operators or handlers') (Davidson, 1994).

Exhibition contractors are probably the most mature part of the industry and have existed for many years. Their function is to provide exhibition services of one kind or another, ranging from design and management services for large exhibitions to the provision of relatively simple one-off stands. Some venues in the exhibition field are able to provide in-house services but may rely on exhibition contractors to create and supply complete shell schemes for exhibitions. Given that some parts of the conference market (medical associations, for example) have a long history of organizing combined conference and exhibition events, a number of exhibition contractors also have expertise in conference production. However, some specialize and act as suppliers of modular systems either for hire or for purchase. Essentially the exhibition stand areas prepared for events tend to have two main components: the shell, or framework (which tends to be standard and provided in modular format of specified size, e.g. 2 m × 2 m or 4 m × 2 m etc.) and the display items, including the graphic material: name-board, logos; specialist lighting and related fittings. Exhibition organization varies, but typically, contractors will provide the shells in a venue and individual exhibitors will fill the shells with their own material, displays and staff for the duration of the exhibition. The contractor will then come in and break down the shells and clear the area.

4.4   Event management companies

Event management companies have often grown out of catering providers for conferences and banquets, and have specialized in provision of the complete event. Events may range from product launches and dinner dances to themed and gala evenings. Event management companies tend to be involved in conferencing where the conference organizers have a requirement for incentive events or specialist dinners linked to the conference or where a product launch demands specialist design and innovation, in a similar way to that undertaken by production companies. Taking the case of the need for an incentive evening, such as a themed dinner, the event management company will be capable of providing the expertise for almost any theme the conference organizer may wish to choose. This will include menu preparation, in terms of identifying a suitable menu to go with the theme, and full catering support in food production and service at the event; also, development of the theme to include specialist sets, props and, if necessary, costumes for delegates or guests, and all the range of support requirements from the provision of special effects and lighting to music (live or recorded) and themed entertainment.

The creation of special events of this type is highly complex, and above all, requires extremely careful planning and costing. The choice of theme itself should also be a matter of careful discussion between the event management company and the conference organizer(s). A great deal depends on the venue, the nature of the facilities (such as kitchens and even wash-up areas), size of the venue, its design features, and elements such as the availability of licensing, parking, loading, power and access.

The conference organizer may choose any one of the above 'packaging' organizations, depending on the requirements of each particular conference: Is it solely a meeting? Is there to be an associated exhibition? In some cases it might even be conceivable that all three types of company are needed together; however, this would be rare. Venues often have approved lists of companies with whom they have previously done business, plus their management structure and any special difficulties which working together implies.

4.5   Other external services

The business of conferences is not solely a matter of taking a number of delegates into a room and giving them a presentation for a couple of hours or for a day. While we have acknowledged that the largest number of conferences in the total market tend to have fewer than 30 delegates and may be relatively simple, rather than high profile events, there is still a need for a range of external services, which is surprising in its extent – anything from transport to translation. Of course, not all conferences need all services, most require only one or two, but there are a wide variety of companies whose chief activity is supplying the conference business, and many more whose chief activity may be elsewhere, but for whom the conference business forms a useful contribution.

Accommodation services

It has been noted that hotels are themselves a major part of the conference business, providing over three-quarters of conference venues. Readers should not pre-suppose that this implies all conferences taking place in hotels are therefore residential; this is not the case, and indeed 77 per cent of all conferences are non-residential, in the view of the English Tourist Board (Richards, 1996). Nevertheless hotel accommodation benefits from conference business in two ways: first, directly, by provision of accommodation for in-house conferences; secondly, indirectly, by the provision of accommodation for conferences taking place at other venues (even other hotels).

Conferences are a major source of income for hotels and something in which certain hotels specialize. As well as the hotel industry having tourist-based hotels, business-based hotels and transient hotels (such as lodges), there are also conference hotels. In some cases there is a great deal of congruence between elements of the different markets. It can be seen that the tourist market (peak – summer) and the conference market (peak – winter) are complementary. As a consequence, a number of locations have sought to exploit this congruence between elements of three different markets. Towns such as Harrogate and Brighton benefit from summer tourists and winter conferences – a very convenient balance of business to have, and as true for many individual hotels as it is for resort towns. Even those hotels without major conference facilities of their own will benefit from conferences elsewhere in their area.

For those conference venues that do not have on-site accommodation, such as purpose-built conference centres or municipal venues, where a conference organizer or buyer wishes to have a residential conference, the venue may have an approved list of local hotels it regularly recommends. This system may be informal or it may be formalized through hotels paying commission to have conference delegates referred. In cities or towns where there is a Visitor and Conference Bureau (such as Manchester and Birmingham), the bureau will maintain a service which links not only venues and hotels but provides the other support services too.

Hotels are not the only participants in the accommodation services part of the business. While they tend to provide accommodation for the corporate market, as do residential management centres, the association market is more fragmented in its use of accommodation, as price is often a significant determinant. Hotels may be used, but the association market also uses guest house accommodation, lodges, university and college accommodation and in some cases hostel accommodation such as the larger YMCAs.

Agencies also play a role in the accommodation service part of the business. Booking agencies, be they conference-booking agencies or hotel-booking agencies, account for over 16 per cent of total conference bookings for hotel and 8 per cent of total bookings for purpose-built venues (Richards, 1996). In the case of either type, there may be a need for residential accommodation and this will be booked as part of the agency's conference role.

Catering services

Setting accommodation to one side, the other major input to the conference business is the need for catering. This covers all aspects of refreshment for delegates. We have, so far, pre-supposed that catering at conferences is undertaken either in-house, or by contractors permanently employed at the venue. There is a third category, and that is the provision of catering services both on an ad hoc basis at venues and as a support externally. A venue might not be able to provide specialist catering for an event which covers both delegates and their partners and for which a larger venue may be needed nearby or for which (for example) a marquee has been requested. It is also the case that in some types of venue, such as a municipal venue, any catering operator may go in to provide the service contracted, perhaps to just one conference.

Catering operators range in size and in the types of service they provide. Events management companies were mentioned earlier as sometimes having developed from catering operators. Equally a number of contract caterers (sometimes called 'outside caterers') have divisions with a specific remit for conference catering. The larger contract catering companies may also run the in-house services of a number of venues and also run ad hoc provision for conferences, exhibitions and other events, including corporate hospitality at arenas or specialist shows. Independent caterers also have a share of the ad hoc conference business (tending to be for the association rather than the corporate market). Also, in the price-restricted part of the association market, there are small independent caterers who provide basic, but sound, catering for conferences in the form of buffets. This type of catering for small association events may be unserviced, that is to say the food/drink is delivered with disposable plates etc., and the conference organizer simply lays it out for delegates to eat. Bakeries often provide this kind of unserviced buffet, simply delivered and paid for on the spot and perfectly adequate for the job.

Technical services

In addition to catering, technical services may also be bought in. Not all venues have the technical support or equipment to cope with the full range of services sometimes demanded by conference organizers. Indeed, the small guest house, hotel or village hall used by parts of the association market may have no facilities at all beyond the room and the furniture. Equipment and technical support can be hired in from a range of companies, some simply providinng equipment, and others providing equipment, training and technical support. Basic presentation equipment can be hired in, ranging from overhead projectors to slide projectors and video players. Most large towns will also have companies capable of making 35 mm slides and computer generated graphics. The higher levels of technology can also be hired in to provide complete presentations on anything from multimedia to video walls. Print shops are capable of copying both black and white and colour material for delegate packs and support material such as badges and name cards. Video production companies are also common and are used not only for producing videos for conferences but also for videoing the conference proceedings themselves, those companies often having their own recording, sound editing and production facilities. The range of technical facilities provided by the companies in this field is extremely wide and reflects the importance that conference organizers, particularly of high profile conferences, attach to the need for technical facilities, whether those facilities are a simple overhead projector, computer-video or liquid crystal display (LCD) projection, prompting systems (autocues) or any other of a wide range of systems to support the speaker.

Transport and guiding services

The transport of delegates to and from conferences can be identified as one of the factors that determine venue buyers' choice of location. It is a common, but probably incorrect, assumption that most delegates travel to conference venues by private car (implying also that conference venues must be capable of providing adequate parking facilities, which must be safe and secure). However, the nature of national and regional conferences, the former in particular, is such that many delegates must use public transport, and thus air, rail and coach accessibility to venues is important. This does not necessarily mean conference venues should be adjacent to transport terminals, merely that they should be accessible from them. In some cases, though, certain venues clearly benefit from their proximity to ter-minii (indeed 'airside' conference facilities are sometimes found at airports, ensuring that international delegates do not have to pass through customs).

Related to the issue of transport to and from venues and transport terminals are the issues of venue/hotel transfers and also travel, as part of a conference or as an incentive 'package' to visit some other attraction. In the case of venue/terminal and venue/hotel transfers the nature of transport provision varies, depending on proximity. Delegates may be able to walk, or taxi services may be appropriate and may be provided formally or informally. Formal agreements are made between a venue and one or more cab companies, perhaps involving some commission; informally any cab will do. There are many venues, in all categories, where transport is a significant issue for delegates not arriving by private car. In such cases the venue (such as a country house hotel) may operate a free courtesy coach/minibus to the nearest railhead or airport at regular intervals or when required. At the top end of this scale would be the provision of chauffeur-driven executive cars to deal with VIPs, though proba-bly only at the request and expense of the conference organizer. For large parties, coaches may be hired; these typically range from 18 to 52 seats and may be luxury vehicles with on-board WCs, drinks, video facilities and host/hostess guides. Coach hire of this kind is particularly useful for both executive travel and for transfers of large numbers of delegates (say, for international delegates arriving by air to a conference). Coach companies do specialize, and a number have conferences as one of their largest markets, not only in terms of transfers but also in terms of tours for partners and incentive travel.

Other support services

Venue buyers and conference organizers may require specialist ser-vices of one kind or another which may have to be bought in, hired or supplied by an agency. For example, most purpose-built venues and many large hotels provide business centres which handle word processing, copying, faxing, and other administrative functions. Support of this kind may be obtained from agencies and a number of conference service companies. Particular conferences may need anything from toastmasters to translation services, and again all are generally available, either through organizations such as visitor and conference bureaux or directly. Translation services are more often provided by purpose-built venues, where if 'real time' translation is necessary, the venue has sound booths available and built-in sound systems for delegates. However, translation can also be a matter not of 'real time' activities but of the translation of scripts and conference papers. Some translation agencies can provide both, together with the necessary equipment; some can only provide one or the other. A number of the larger purpose-built venues also provide support services which are uncommon at other venues. These include medical services, such as a nurse on duty during daytime hours or crèche facilities. These may be provided in-house, on contract or by special request to a company that services them. In the latter two cases, conference venues must take particular care that services are provided only by reputable organizations.

Summary

The increasing complexity of conference presentation has seen the development of companies with specialist roles on the production side of the conference business; some of these companies, such as exhibition contractors, have been around for many years; some, such as conference production companies and events management companies are a relatively recent type of specialized activity. Further, many conference venues are too small to provide all the services that delegates or organizers require; therefore, various companies provide specialist support from catering to accommodation, from technical equipment to transport. All are components in the final product.

References

Davidson, R. (1994) *Business Travel*, London, Pitman, pp. 32–38.
GMVB (1996) *Conference and Exhibition Guide 1996*, Manchester, Greater Manchester Visitor and Convention Bureau.
Goldblatt, J.J. (1990) *Special Events*, New York, Van Nostrand Reinhold, pp. 17–28.
Konopka, C. (1995) The Big Event. *Caterer and Hotelkeeper*, 18 May, pp. 64–66.
Kotas, R. and Jayawardena, C. (1994) *Profitable Food and Beverage Management*, London, Hodder and Stoughton, pp.192–235.

Richards, B. (1992) *How to Market Tourist Attractions, Festivals and Special Events*, Harlow, Longman, pp. 101–110.

Richards, B. (1996) The Conference Market in the UK. In *Insights*, March, London, English Tourist Board, pp. B67–B83.

Part Two _____

Facilities and Services _____

5

Conference and meeting areas

The aims of this chapter are:

1 To explore who the stakeholders are in the process of conference area design and to identify the objectives of providing conference facilities in terms of delegate needs.
2 To identify the major aspects of design of conference areas, in terms of the conference room itself; what elements are involved, both physically and intangibly; design aspects of networking areas and issues of servicing, safety and security.

5.1   Introduction

Conference venues are not always purpose-built; many are converted from buildings whose primary function was not that of conferences. As a consequence, some venues are remarkably unsuited to their job. There are three groups (of stakeholders) who should influence the design of conference areas: architects, operators and delegates. Their aims may not always be mutually congruent. However, as crucial to the issue of conference area design as 'who' it is designed for, is the purpose of a conference venue. It is necessary to start at the purpose and work outwards. A conference has several roles, both formal and informal: exchange of ideas; enhancement of communication as a leadership forum; recognition of participants; networking; providing a vehicle for hidden agendas. In addition to these functions, we must bear in mind that a conference venue often has a role in the local community, whether that role is understood in its 'micro' sense, such as being a place to get a coffee or providing some community function, maybe a destination for a school field trip, perhaps a venue for a 'pro bono' event (providing a place for a charity Christmas dinner for local pensioners, for example); or in the 'macro' sense of providing the community with economic and social benefits such as employment (or the design may need to fit in with other nearby buildings etc. – the 'macro' environment).

Many conference venues are poorly designed, partly, maybe, because of the constraints of their existing buildings, partly, perhaps, because of the lack of awareness of the venue's management of the need to consider the full implications of design decisions. The purpose of this reading is simply to provide an overview. For a more detailed insight to design the reader should refer in the first place to Lawson (1995) and thereafter to authors and practitioners on building design. Key issues are:

- access, external circulation (arrival and departure) and internal circulation around the venue;
- ambience, the quality of the interior in terms of comfort, lighting, warmth, colour, furniture and general fixtures and fittings;
- lighting;
- air conditioning;
- noise, internal and external;
- servicing, the provision of adequate support areas for activities such as catering and housekeeping;
- safety and security;
- the provision of technology, including presentation and computer systems.

The issue of the standard of design of conference areas can often show itself, not in elements of good design, but in those elements that go wrong. Experience would suggest that delegates have an awareness of the things that work well in a conference venue – indeed where things work well they are largely ignored. A venue can expect little thanks for the efficiency of its air conditioning system if it works properly but many complaints if it does not. Delegates may well argue that an excellent venue was one where they noticed nothing whatever about the systems. To a certain extent, particularly in design, this may lead to blandness, but the counter-argument would be that it is better for delegates not to notice anything of the design features rather than come out of the room complaining about bad lighting, squeaky chairs and claustrophobia. Nevertheless, good design should achieve efficiency, but should also, probably, give a feeling for the venue and its surroundings, however intangible, to help ensure that delegates wish to return.

5.2 The objectives of conference areas

Three principal groups have an interest in the development of conference areas: the designers (or architects), the operators and the users (or delegates). These three groups are often seen as being somewhat at odds. The architect of the Lloyds Building in London (Richard Rogers) was lauded by his profession for creating a building which was unique and 'modern'. However, 75 per cent of the users indicated that they would prefer to return to their former building across the street (Becker, 1995). The operators have had to spend significant additional amounts of money making changes, though the architect argued that all his plans were approved by Lloyds. It is of some interest to find, therefore, that the International Convention Centre (ICC) in Birmingham won the 'wooden spoon' in the 1991 Sunday Times Architecture Awards, but surveys of user attitudes towards the ICC found a good general level of acceptance of facilities (Foxall and Hackett, 1994).

When considering the range of published work addressing the issue of facilities for meetings and conferences, it is evident that there is a concentration on 'how' a room is laid out for the meeting itself, rather than design. While this is laudable and necessary, it reflects an archaic and narrow view of the purpose of conferences, that is to say the event only serves to exchange information in a formal setting. Clearly this fails to recognize other important functions. A conference has several roles (Woods and Berger 1988), noted earlier, and each has a design implication:

- **The generation and exchange of information and ideas** This is the most crucial element and generally the chief reason for holding conferences, many of which have an educational or training role.
- **The enhancement of communication** Clarity of communication is considered to be a significant outcome of conferences – where the communication may, for example, be much more direct from managers to staff than in the normal workplace environment; thus communication is improved and helps create shared knowledge and values.

- **The development of recognition and unity**   This is partly an internal issue, partly an external one. Internally, it is the need for a delegate to have some recognition and support from peers and superiors, thereby helping to develop a spirit of unity and corporate identity. Externally, it may be that an organization is sending a delegate to a conference in order to be recognized as a contributor in that field.
- **As a leadership forum**   A conference or convention may be one of the few opportunities for people in large organizations to see their leadership in action; as such the conference is an opportunity for managers to act visibly as leaders at this type of event and to promote or explain their aims.
- **To create commitment to a common goal**   Where an organization wishes to involve more of its members in decision making, thus obtaining their commitment to that process.
- **Networking**   This is also crucial to the conference business. The ability to meet people, make new contacts and discuss issues on an informal basis is often seen as the most productive part of a conference: 'The speaker was terrible, but I met Mark from publicity and we've got this idea …'.
- **The exploration of hidden agendas**   Whatever the 'official' reasons for attending a conference, there will also be unofficial ones, these may have as much to do with the location of the conference (e.g. in a city well known for its excellent shopping) as with personal issues (e.g. an opportunity to meet old friends), or any number of other, subtler reasons.

It can be seen from these roles that the design and arrangement of conference rooms is only half the task, the other half is to support or maximize the opportunities for networking, interaction, socializing, conversation and reflection.

5.3   Design aspects of conference areas

Think, now, of some of the conferences or meetings or lectures you have attended, the rooms these have taken place in, and how this has affected your view of the conference itself. Think of all those rooms with no natural light, low ceilings and stuffy atmospheres. Think of the claustrophobia, the inertia, the disinterest to which poor design submits delegates. Think of the confusing layout of many venues, the design of signs by people who don't grasp the importance of accurate waymarking. Think of those uniform nondescript walls of magnolia and those carpets of charmless mud-brown. Or, worse still, think of a delightful venue, open and light, ruined by the ineptitude of the management in their choice of fixtures and fittings: red flock wallpaper on the walls, a green carpet inherited from another venue in the group because it was cheap, blue chairs borrowed from the dining room because, well, 'we aren't really geared up to do conferences this big', and the kind of colour scheme that would shame a Nevada brothel.

What are the issues? The design aspects of conference areas are as crucial to the success of conferences as are the other services, the speakers, the programme and the management. The conference does not start when the first speaker taps the microphone and politely coughs for attention. The conference, from the users' or delegates' viewpoint, starts when they arrive at the venue – at the car park or at reception (Rutes and Penner, 1985).

Access

How do delegates generally arrive at the venue? By car, by air or rail? On foot? It is necessary to consider all these things. Is the access easy? Is it easy to find? Is it clearly evident by its design, by its signposting, by its lighting? Is the car park adequate, easy to use, clean and safe? Car parks should at least have good lighting and feel safe for delegates. These are the users' issues. What about the operators? Ease of access is equally important, particularly to loading areas for (potentially) very large vehicles. Internally, access issues relate to both people and goods. Are there public routes and service routes? What are the crush points or traffic nodes? What routes exist in case of emergency? What routes are suitable for disabled people?

Layout

In so far as the issues of access are relevant to the exterior of a venue, these are also true of interior access, or circulation. Here, the points made earlier about networking and the careful consideration of layouts to facilitate networking also apply, but need to be looked at bearing in mind the needs of safety and egress in case of emergency, and the specific layout requirements to allow for circulation of delegates within a building, where there are also traffic flows (of people) and servicing needs. As much as the outside of a building could be gridlocked by bad exit (or entrance) design, so the interior of a building can be equally overwhelmed by large numbers of people assembling for, or exiting from, a conference. (See Figure 5.1.)

Ambience

Conference organizers are not only looking for a pleasant location in an external sense, they are also looking for a pleasant location in the internal sense. In some cases, where there are issues of corporate image, this will be of considerable importance. This may lead to venue managers opting for relatively plain interiors so as not to 'distract' delegates; while this is justifiable and understandable, there is a need to avoid the 'could be anywhere' blandness of many venues. How does the venue represent itself, its location and its history – can these elements be used to improve the ambience or give a flavour of the surroundings? Conference rooms should be comfortable and have some elements of flexibility for users, particularly in the control of lighting, heating and ventilation. Ambience is developed not only through the careful use of interior decor, colour, lighting and warmth, but also through the choice of furniture, linen, flowers, table elements (such as pads, water glasses etc.), pictures and other fixtures and fittings.

Lighting

Conference rooms depend on artificial lighting, though some are well enough lit by natural light. The lighting provision has to satisfy both background (general) light requirements and the task lighting needed for particular issues such as lighting a speaker, being sufficiently adjustable to allow for technical presentations, being controllable from more than one location in a room; in general, being sufficiently flexible for a range of conference tasks.

Air conditioning

Conference rooms may also depend on air conditioning in addition to, or in place of, natural ventilation. There are two chief problems with air conditioning: first, the lack of local control, which often

Figure 5.1 Example of the floorplan of a conference area

leads to discomfort in a particular room if the controls are preset to the needs of another part of the building; secondly, the noise which accompanies many air conditioning systems, so much so that conference delegates often prefer to be too hot rather than be unable to listen to the proceedings due to the noise of the air conditioning system.

Noise

Related to air conditioning noise is noise in general. Conferences are frequently disrupted by exterior noise, maintenance noise (e.g. drilling), aircraft noise, noise from emergency vehicles outside and so on. Noise pollution is an increasing problem, some of it from sources which have questionable value, such as car alarms. Conference venues can seek to reduce external noise by careful design but this cannot always deal with noise generated internally due to maintenance or the setting up of another room nearby. Conference venue managers should take reasonable care in scheduling to try to obviate noise, though the issue may well be venue-specific (some venues have a particular noise problem, some have not). Poor design of interconnecting room partitions is one such issue. Poor original design (such as an echo) may be another. Noise also has to be considered from the opposite viewpoint, i.e. is the conference room creating noise which interferes with another part of the building (particularly in hotels) or another conference? This is also an issue of noise containment as well as the reduction of over-enthusiastic use of sound reinforcement (public address systems) by conference speakers.

Intangibles

The blandness of many conference venues mentioned earlier, the magnolia walls, the ignorable curtains, the delicately coloured pictures of Monsieur Montgolfier's balloons on the walls, may be necessary to ensure delegates can concentrate on the presentations and on the quality of the debate, but these things should not be so vacuous as to eliminate all sense of personality and intimacy from a venue. After all the design effort which may go into a venue, to ensure the lighting works, the furniture is comfortable and the delegates can see the overhead projection, the design should also serve to encourage organizers and delegates to return. It was of much interest, and some controversy, that when the International Convention Centre was built in Birmingham, 1 per cent of expenditure was devoted to public art. The quality of some of the art has been questioned, but the reasoning is sound. A venue should be attractive, and it should have sufficient of its own personality to help encourage repeat business among delegates, conference organizers and agents.

5.4   Design aspects of networking areas

Interaction at conferences can be considered in a number of ways – official or unofficial, group or individual, formal or informal. The arrangement of conference areas has to be capable of supporting this. Is interaction facilitated or hindered at breaks? Are there areas for groups to assemble? Is there scope for individuals to work and for quiet reflection? Or, is it the case that once a plenary session breaks, the entire mass of seething humanity who have been in the conference room are simply deposited in a corridor at a break? A corridor that has to serve as circulating area, rest area and as a cramped place to queue an inordinately long time for a cup of tepid coffee and a selection of dry biscuits (and then not have time to talk with the Vice-President).

Even in those buildings which are not purpose designed, it should still be within the ingenuity of management to make adequate arrangements for elementary service functions and for the flow of people, and also to provide for convivial and useful social interaction of delegates. The planning process must not stop at 'what layout is required in the conference room?'. It must contribute and include:

● An understanding of traffic flows: when a conference breaks the delegates may first head for the toilets, then back for coffee or for lunch or to network. Where are the crunch points, where are the cross-flows, where are the quiet spots in the design?
● An understanding that corridors are probably inadequate places to serve coffee/buffets or set up stands.
● An understanding that the networking function has to have adequate space, and a balance of group areas and places where individuals can interact, both standing and sitting.

Once a conference venue has had to design for networking as well as formal activity, it should also become an integral part of the pre-planning of an event.

The network styles can vary, but the effective use of informal seating/tables/screens and planters is as important to the delegates getting the most out of a conference as is having good speakers or presenters. The objective is to generate contacts between the delegates. Even the location of the table from which the coffee is served may well have an impact on effective communication, interplay and contact.

5.5   Servicing, safety and security

From the viewpoint of an operator, the most important need is to be able to service a conference efficiently; however, particularly in hotels, the design and availability of service areas are often inadequate for the job. This is particularly the case with furniture and equipment stores and with service kitchen facilities. It is necessary to consider, in the design of conference venues, how the conference rooms are to be serviced. The elements are:

- Lay up and breakdown of furniture (transport and storage).
- Lay up and breakdown of technical equipment (transport and storage).
- Cleaning and housekeeping of rooms (transport and storage of cleaning equipment, linen and consumable items).
- Provision of refreshments (availability of service or 'holding' kitchens for food, temporary or permanent bars, dispense areas and still rooms for hot beverage preparation).

Sometimes, in purpose-designed venues, these functions are carried out from a service core, which also contains lifts, circulating areas, toilets, stairways, a business centre, foyers, cloakrooms etc. Careful design of the service core may well reduce staffing requirements; for example, in older hotels particularly, the transport time for moving equipment or refreshments from the nearest service area or kitchen to a conference room may be significant and wasteful (Lawson, 1995).

The physical issues of safety and security are particularly relevant to buildings which are essentially public. Conference venues and hotels are open places and people cannot be prevented from entering the public areas, nor would we wish to prevent them. It is important that visitors and delegates are at ease in conference venues, that they do not feel spied upon or feel that they are the subject of interference with their personal freedom. Indeed it is useful and productive to encourage the public to see venues; we do not expect them to go into the meeting rooms (and this is the level at which some oversight is needed), but we would encourage them to use, say, a coffee shop area/entrance foyer, as a means of promoting our venues, and also be able to see venues as part of an official tour or open day to develop community relations (Croner Publications, 1992).

Baseline security is generally in the hands of security officers, or in venues too small to justify full-time security, a member of the management with a security responsibility. Video cameras are a common sight around buildings and at entrances in particular. While these may be controlled by a central security office, in smaller venues and in hotels they may be monitored in reception. Emergency procedures and evacuation routines are also important and design must take into account ease of exit in case of emergency and fire prevention, containment, control and alarm. Larger conference venues may also have design provision for a medical/first-aid room.

Summary

The good design of buildings is always going to be a matter of subjective opinion; however, in the past, the emphasis in design of conference venues has always been on the formal, and has neglected the informal activities of networking and social interaction. As much as the modern conference venue needs to have well-designed meeting rooms, supply areas and good circulation, it also needs to provide areas for informal discussion and quiet reflection.

References

Becker, F. (1995) *The Total Workplace*, New York, Van Nostrand Reinhold, pp. 175–179.

Croner Publications (1992) *A Practical Approach to the Administration of Leisure and Recreation Services*, London, Croner Publications, 4th edn, pp. 155–205, 257–287.

Duffy, F. (1990) *The Responsive Office*, Streatley, Polymath, pp. 40–46.

Foxall, G. and Hackett, P. (1994) Consumer Satisfaction with Birmingham's International Convention Centre. *The Service Industries Journal*, **14**(3), July, pp. 369–380.

Goldblatt, J.J. (1990) *Special Events, The Art and Science of Celebration*, New York, Van Nostrand Reinhold, pp. 299–309.

Lawson, F. (1981) *Conference, Convention and Exhibition Facilities*, London, Architectural Press, pp. 115–149, 158–169.

Lawson, F. (1995) *Hotels and Resorts, Planning, Design and Refurbishment*, Oxford, Butterworth-Heinemann, (a) pp. 251–264, (b) pp. 274–291.

Rutes, W.A. and Penner, R.H. (1985) *Hotel Planning and Design*, London, Architectural Press, pp. 87–97.

Woods, R.H. and Berger, F. (1988) Making Meetings Work. *Cornell Hotel and Restaurant Quarterly*, **29**, pp. 101–105.

6

The provision of food and drink

The aims of this chapter are:

1 To explain the chief means by which conference venues organize the catering of events.
2 To understand the information required by caterers to provide conference delegates with appropriate meals and service.
3 To discuss the types of service on offer to conference delegates in terms of refreshment breaks and drinks services.

6.1   Introduction

Having provided a suitably laid out meeting room for delegates, the issue which will probably most colour their view of the conference itself, if not the venue, is the provision of food and drink. This chapter will look at some of the practicalities of catering for conferences. Refreshment breaks not only provide opportunities for delegates to deal with their personal needs, make phone calls, check out baggage and so on, but are also the chief mechanism by which conference delegates network and socialize. Refreshment breaks and meals are significant factors in determining the quality of the venue and delegates' perception of it, and a major issue in ensuring repeat business (Kotas and Jayawardena, 1994).

The organization of catering varies considerably depending on the type of venue, but, as a generality, there is a fairly clear split between in-house catering as practised by the conference and banqueting departments of hotel venues and contracted-out catering as practised by other types of venue, ranging from purpose-built conference centres to management training centres. There are advantages and disadvantages to both methods of organization, and the type provided by venues to handle their catering may have as much to do with historical precedent in that venue as with matters of profitability, flexibility and convenience which are the normal issues at hand in the debate about in-house versus contracted-out provision.

Having found a caterer, of whatever type, the basic questions and the starting points to determine what the delegate will have are the same. These are questions of the number of people, of refreshment times, of the budget and of the delegates themselves. It could be argued that one of the chief failings of catering provision at conferences is an insensitivity towards the type of delegates a conference may bring. There is a tendency towards standardized menus which, while convenient for chefs and conference sales co-ordinators, may be inappropriate for certain delegates. Increasingly, delegates are better educated in food and drink than at any time in the past, an issue which was well illustrated during the UK beef crisis of 1996, where some slow-moving conference venues were still pushing out standard menus with beef dishes to conference organizers who were rejecting them with hard words.

The range of services on offer is essentially built around five main refreshment opportunities: breakfast, morning coffee, lunch, afternoon tea and dinner. These are not the only opportunities. It is possible to offer conference delegates working breakfasts, brunches and, in the North of England, especially in Lancashire and Yorkshire, high teas as alternatives, depending on the time structure of a conference. In terms of drinks service, a typical non-residential conference may only extend to a glass of wine or orange juice with the buffet lunch; but for residential conferences, and in particular those that may feature a gala dinner (see Figure 6.1 for an example), there is clearly an opportunity to encourage drink sales at the pre-dinner reception and after dinner for residents, most often through the provision of a cash bar.

The final key issue regarding meals, in particular, is that of menu composition. This is significant not only in terms of the design of standard menus (see Figure 6.3 for an example), but also where a conference venue may offer a variation of the à la carte system, that is to say a range of individually priced dishes which are suggested to the conference organizer who then chooses a set menu for delegates from the available dishes (see Figure 6.4 for an example). This is based on the view that conference organizers know something of the style, likes and dislikes of the delegates. However, not all do, and

SHORELINE CONFERENCE CENTRE

Gala Dinner Menu
Annual Conference of East Anglian Windsurfers

Cream of courgette and green peppercorn soup
Creme potage de courgette et grains de poivre vert

or

Broccoli and prawns in oyster sauce
Brocoli et crevettes roses sauce huitre

∞

Baked breast of duck served with raspberry sauce
Supreme de canard foure et sauce framboises

or

Poached fillet of salmon served with drambuie and lobster sauce
filet de saumon poche servir un sauce de drambuie et homard

or

Spicy potato roulade with salad Raita
Roulade de pommes Bombay et salad de concombre, yogurt et menthe
Served with a selection of potatoes and fresh vegetables
Tous accompagne de pommes et legumes fraiche

∞

Chocolate and malt whisky parfait
Parfait de chocolat Glenlivet

or

A light lemon sorbet
Sorbet au citron

∞

Coffee and marzipan bites
Cafe avec petits fours

Guest of honour: Andrew Morton-Gray,
National President of the Windsurfers Association

12th May 1997

Figure 6.1 Example of a conference gala dinner menu (delegates choose prior to dinner)

organizers often pick dishes they themselves like, only to find that delegates criticize their poor judgement. Menu composition is, therefore, not simply a technical issue, but also one of the most appropriate questions that conference organizers can ask themselves, i.e. what are their delegates' food preferences?

6.2   Food and drink organization

There are two main methods of provision in terms of food and drink at conference venues: in-house and contracted (or 'outsourced'). In-house provision is done by the organization itself as part of its core operation. This is chiefly how hotels operate (Medlik, 1995). The banqueting department of a hotel provides food and drink for all the functions and events that take place within the establishment.

Each organization is different, but the chief 'back of house' players are the Head Chef and the Bars Manager, in the sense that they are responsible for food and drink costings, pre-planning, ordering and preparation of food and drink. Nevertheless, it must be remembered that the initial enquiry and first meeting between the venue and the conference organizer will probably take place with the venue sales manager or conference sales co-ordinator, though a number of conference organizers will ask for the chef to be present.

The alternative is to contract out the catering to a specialist organization (Warner, 1989). Such organizations vary from the large national operations with many contracts to small individual caterers with only one contract. Outsourced catering of this kind is common in purpose-built conference venues, municipal venues, some educational establishments and some specialist venues. Contractual arrangements vary. Some venues may have one approved caterer who provides all the food, drink and related services for that venue. Such contracts are often time limited, e.g. five years. Alternatively, some venues may have an 'approved' list of caterers with whom they are happy to work, the caterers being familiar with the venue, its operation and management and typical requirements. A very few venues, such as public halls, may allow any caterer, but this is uncommon.

The advantage of contracting-out is that the venue does not need to concern itself with the technicalities of food and drink provision; it simply makes the best contractual arrangement possible, sometimes on a commission basis, and merely acts as a link between the conference organizer and the caterers. The disadvantage is loss of control: in a contract which lasts five years, a contract caterer interested in cutting costs may have no incentive to provide a quality service, only providing it towards the end of the contract on the basis that the venue management may have a short memory and will happily renew the contract for a further five years. The related disadvantage in terms of 'loss of control' is less well known, but probably more serious – loss of flexibility. The in-house catering function is, in practice, highly flexible and can provide peripheral activities which contractors do not. The chief problem is that contracts are often badly written, ignoring a wide range of needs, some of which may only occur occasionally but are nevertheless vital, and for which a contractor will charge extra.

6.3   Basic issues in the provision of food and drink

The starting point for the provision of food and drink is the nature of the conference itself. Clearly a residential conference will require a greater food and drink input than a non-residential conference; similarly a VIP conference will require a greater level of input and service than, say, an association or charity conference might. There are several key questions for the caterer which will determine the arrangements for food and drink – see Figure 6.2.

The number of delegates attending and expected to eat may not be the same, particularly for residential breakfasts or conference dinners. It is also of some importance to have approximate numbers

---

- The number of delegates attending and expected to eat

- The times of refreshment breaks and meals

- Details about the delegates themselves:

  - Who they are
  - Typical interests
  - Age group
  - Male/female balance
  - Special dietary needs (e.g. vegetarians)

- The budget for refreshments

- The expertise and ability of the catering staff

Figure 6.2   Issues in determining menus and refreshments

(give or take 10 per cent) up to two weeks prior to the event and final numbers two days in advance to enable not only accurate food and drink ordering but also satisfactory table lay-ups. Last-minute number checks for refreshments can be made as the conference is taking place. The time of refreshment breaks should also be checked with the organizers on the day, as the originally scheduled time may vary depending on circumstances (Seekings, 1996).

The budget for refreshments is generally pre-determined from the beginning. It is common for conference organizers to choose from a range of pre-priced set menus or from a list of possible dishes from which an appropriate menu can be made up and costed (see Figure 6.4). If the clients wish to have a special meal prepared for the 'end of conference' dinner, the planning of such a meal should take into account the background of the delegates (a conference of medical practitioners may not appreciate a high cholesterol meal) and their interests – are the delegates, for example, outdoor activity enthusiasts and if so how would this impinge on the menu composition? Other issues are the age group of the delegates: younger people may, for example, be particularly averse to red meat dishes, more so than an older age group. What is the balance of male to female delegates? What proportion are likely to be vegetarian? (This latter is an increasingly serious issue, many conference delegates who are not themselves vegetarian may be quite happy to take the vegetarian dish rather than the main dish on offer (Davis and Stone, 1991).

For many years, the food on offer at conference dinners and formal banquets was extremely predictable. A standard fare of prawn cocktail, chicken in sauce and sherry trifle was almost inevitable. Even today, it would be possible for delegates to find common 'set meals' including an indeterminate pâté, a badly cooked rack of lamb (a recent trend, and bearing in mind the incidence of food poisoning, a deplorable one) and a sweet comprising a brandy snap basket with ice cream on a pool of red berry juice. Conference delegates may be conservative (i.e. traditional) in their tastes, but they are no longer uneducated in food. Travel abroad, ethnic restaurants at home and wide-ranging food programmes and articles in the media have engendered a far greater range of tastes in the UK and Irish public. Conference venues and hotels are not always in the forefront of change when developing menus, nor perhaps would delegates necessarily wish them to be; but it is entirely necessary that the food presented at conferences is of a high standard. Frequently it is not, and part of the reason for this is the lack of competitor analysis (what in other industries would be called benchmarking), and compla-

SHORELINE CONFERENCE CENTRE

Finger Buffet: Menu A

Spicy potato wedges with a trio of dips
Stilton and garlic mushrooms
Chinese marinaded chicken wings
Brie and spinach barquettes
Essex smoked ham and asparagus
   roulades
A selection of finger sandwiches

Fork Buffet: Menu B

Honeydew melon with a mango sorbet
or
Cream of farmhouse vegetable soup

∾

Breast of Norfolk turkey & chestnut
   stuffing
or
Honey glazed gammon ham
or
Poached salmon with lemon mayon-
   naise
with
Various salads: Coleslaw; Potato;
   Waldorf
Hot buttered Jersey potatoes

∾

Oranges in caramel
or
Viennese cherry and kirsch torte

∾

Coffee or Tea

Set Dinner: Menu C

Fantasy of seasonal melon on a raspberry coulis

∾

Supreme of chicken with a wild mushroom and whisky sauce
Chef's selection of fresh market vegetables and potato

∾

A rich dark and white chocolate mousse

∾

Coffee and mints

Figure 6.3 Examples of various conference menu styles

SHORELINE CONFERENCE CENTRE

Starters: A choice from:
OAK SMOKED SALMON WITH DILL SAUCE
MISCELLANY OF SEAFOOD ON SHREDDED LETTUCE TOPPED WITH A LEMON DRESSING
CHEF'S SMOOTH CHICKEN LIVER PATE
TERRINE OF PORK AND APPLE
FANNED HONEYDEW MELON ON A PASSION FRUIT COULIS
MELON PEARLS, FLAVOURED WITH PORT
HOT MUSHROOM TART WITH A FRENCH MUSTARD GLAZE
FRUITS OF THE FOREST SORBET
COLCHESTER OYSTERS WITH BROWN BREAD

Soups: A choice from:
CREAM OF LEEK AND POTATO SOUP
CREAM SOLFERINO
FRENCH ONION SOUP WITH PARMESAN CHEESE GALETTES
CREAM OF CROMER CRAB SOUP

Main Courses: A choice from:
PAUPIETTE OF SOLE WITH PRAWNS AND LOBSTER SAUCE
POACHED DELICE OF SALMON IN A WHITE WINE BOUILLON
POACHED SUPREME OF CHICKEN WITH A WHITE WINE AND MUSHROOM SAUCE
ROAST LEG OF LAMB GLAZED WITH A REDCURRANT JUS
INDIVIDUAL BEEF WELLINGTON WITH MADEIRA SAUCE
ESCALOPE OF PORK WITH A LEMON AND ORANGE GLAZE
SUPREME OF PHEASANT WITH STILTON AND PORT SAUCE
OSTRICH STEAK WITH A CREAM, BRANDY AND PEPPERCORN SAUCE
VEGETARIAN MUSHROOM STROGANOFF WITH WILD RICE
VEGETARIAN BAKED STUFFED RED PEPPER WITH ONION GRAVY

ALL SERVED WITH FRESH GARDEN VEGETABLES AND POTATOES

Sweets: A choice from:
A RICH CHOCOLATE AND MALT WHISKY PARFAIT
APPLE AND FRANGIPANE TART WITH VANILLA SAUCE
RASPBERRIES IN COINTREAU FLAVOURED CREAM, WITH LIGHT SPONGE FINGERS
OLD ENGLISH WINTER SPOTTED DICK WITH CUSTARD SAUCE
SHORTBREAD FILLED WITH A STRAWBERRY AND GRAND MARNIER CREAM
A LIGHT CITRUS SORBET
SHORELINE'S SPECIAL FRESH FRUIT SALAD IN SPRING WATER SYRUP WITH CALVADOS

Cheeses:
SELECTION OF ENGLISH CHEESES
SELECTION OF CONTINENTAL CHEESES

Coffees:
COFFEE WITH CREAM AND MINT CHOCOLATES
COFFEE WITH CREAM AND BELGIAN TRUFFLES
A SELECTION OF FINE TEAS CAN ALSO BE PROVIDED

Figure 6.4   Example of a conference menu suggestion list – the final menu may be selected from a range

cency on the part of venues. Older banqueting managers may recall the days when it was de rigueur to go out and eat in competitor establishments, hotels particularly. This is now extremely rare among modern managers and the quality of conference food sometimes suffers from the lack of knowledge of what competitors are providing (Venison, 1983). There are other common weaknesses in conference dining, some of which are training related. Conference dining often relies on casual waiting staff and this is a particular difficulty. Such staff have often gleaned their meagre knowledge of service from other staff or from ad hoc demonstrations by the head waiter or waitress. The days of finding one's entire banqueting staff consuming the remains of the conference's sherry trifle in the back room of the banqueting kitchen are not yet gone. Would that such concerted effort went into training or even that it were applied to a half-hour briefing before service about the food, the drink, whom to serve first and how to look around for delegates and diners trying to attract staff attention.

The final issue is the feeding of staff and crew. In the effort to cut costs, the feeding of staff is generally neglected, but nevertheless should be a charge supported as part of the total, either calculated into menu prices or added as a specific budgeting line. How many staff and crew need to be fed, with what, at what time and by whom? Will the staff dining room be open, if there is one? Do staff and crew pay for reasonable refreshments in such a dining room? If not, where and how are the staff and crew to be fed?

6.4 Food and drink services

The simplest form of conference will, at some point, involve the consumption of food and drink. A day conference may typically take the format shown in Figure 6.5. For a residential conference, two other meal opportunities can be added: breakfast and the conference dinner. There are, of course, many variations on this type of schedule, depending on the nature of the meeting, its purpose, the delegates, even the location. The day may start earlier with a working breakfast and end with lunch. Certain types of service are common at conferences, however: breakfast is generally a buffet breakfast with both hot and cold dishes, and delegates may therefore choose for themselves whether to have a full cooked breakfast or go for something more continental. In hotels it will also be highly likely that delegates will take breakfast (unless it is a working breakfast) with all the other hotel guests.

08.45 a.m.	Coffee on arrival, check in
09.00 a.m.	First session
11.00 a.m.	Morning coffee and pastries
11.15 a.m.	Second session
1.00 p.m.	Buffet lunch
2.00 p.m.	Third session
3.30 p.m.	Afternoon tea with biscuits
5.00 p.m.	End

Figure 6.5   Example refreshment schedule of a day conference

'Morning coffee' is shorthand for 'morning coffee or tea', usually with biscuits or small cakes such as miniature Danish pastries. Conference venues must not make the mistake of believing that 'morning coffee' refers to coffee only; this is a regrettably common mistake, but a stupid one.

Lunch for conference delegates often has two major prerequisites: first, that it should be relatively light, normally a main course and a sweet; secondly, that it should be brief – to be accomplished in an hour. There are two common types of service – served lunch or buffet lunch. The latter is far more common and itself may be sub-divided into two types: finger buffet or fork buffet. With the former, delegates would normally stand, with the latter (again the more common), delegates would normally sit – the buffet food may be hot or cold or both. The timing issue is an important one. The British and the Irish will politely queue at a buffet, but this will increase the time and must be taken into account when laying a buffet. More than one direction or side of a buffet table should be available. It will take the average delegate 20 seconds to load his/her plate – multiply that up by the number of delegates and you will understand why more than one buffet flow is needed for a large event. It should also be borne in mind that buffets are often understaffed. This leads to chaos, inability to restock, inability to clear tables and loss of that conference's repeat business. The normal buffet service ratio is one staff to 30 diners. This can be raised to 35 if serving international delegates: they are less likely to queue, and will simply descend on a buffet table and ravage it. This must be noted when laying out the buffet – for international delegates the buffet should not generally be laid out in a linear fashion (Cotterell, 1994).

'Afternoon tea' is shorthand for 'afternoon tea or coffee', usually with biscuits, shortcake, small cakes or scones with jam and clotted cream (depending on the region or locality). Timing is an issue, both at morning coffee and afternoon tea, as sessions may overrun; but, if booked at, say, 3.30 p.m. then the service must be ready at 3.30 p.m. The day this fails to happen is the day the conference breaks on time and thus the 'missing' service causes unnecessary friction between the conference organizer and the floor manager or staff on duty.

Conference dinners are often intended as the highlight of th event, sometimes in the form of gala dinners or theme dinners provide a fitting end (Goldblatt, 1990). Regrettably, they are, often, badly done, with poorly cooked food, indifferent service a poorly presented staff. Service is not a matter of slapping a plate chicken in front of a delegate and standing back. It is as importar this environment as it is in the fine restaurants of great ho Dinner is typically a seated event, with a preset menu, generally little or no choice, except for a gala or special dinner; for smaller ference parties, dinner, particularly in hotels, may be taken fro restaurant menu or from a limited choice table d'hôte However, once numbers exceed 50 or so a preset menu is likely.

This, in theory, should assist the production of a meal of good quality, but often it results in the production of a unimaginative and unappetising meal because the kitchen routine and simple. For a set menu, the typical service rat staff to between 10 and 15 diners, plus one member of di (for wine service) to every 30 diners.

Bars at this type of function should be staffed at a ra member of staff to every 75 drinkers (for example, at the reception). These ratios can be subject to some va instance, experience of a particular residential conferenc clude that delegates, on previous visits, have been partic drinkers, thus requiring a strengthening of the service. tance of this latter point is that the conference and manager responsible for food and drink service at dinner (or lunch, or breakfast) must be flexible. It is assume that a preset standard will do for all functions approach, but leads to lack of attention to the detail potentially serious mistakes such as under- or over-s

Bars at conferences are essentially of two types: Paid bars are those where the conference organizer some element of payment for delegates, let us say V

drinks, because the conference organizer (on behalf of the company or association) is paying. In some cases, conference organizers may specify that delegates may cover their first drink by this method; however, such arrangements must be made clear to delegates and strict monitoring applied. Far better, simply, to serve a pre-determined aperitif (e.g. sherry) than attempt to monitor who is 'just' having their first drink. The alternative method is to set a bar limit, which the organizer will pay for, and after which delegates pay for their own. Again, this method has severe limitations and could result in an undignified scrum at the bar to get as many 'free' ones as possible before delegates have to pay. It is far easier, and much more common, to have a cash bar. Delegates pay for what they have.

There is also the related issue of drinks served during the meal. The most common method is for organizers to include an allowance of one or two glasses of wine or juice with a meal for delegates; thereafter, delegates may buy their own wine on payment to the sommelier (wine waiter/waitress); similarly with liqueurs, which are usually on a cash basis. Drinks service tends to go on the basis of one bottle of wine (75 cl) to six persons with a common ratio of three to one in favour of white to red. Spirit service is of the order of 28 (25 ml) measures to a bottle. Jugged plain water should always be put on the table before the meal arrives. There is a belief that diners will not drink alcohol if water is put on the tables. This belief is fallacious, and it always results in tables asking for water and service being disrupted to get it. Such disruptions delegates can do without.

Cleaning and clearing are issues much neglected in the servicing of conference rooms and at conference meals, particularly buffets. It is essential that when a conference breaks for refreshment or at any other point, the opportunity is taken for minor rubbish clearing, replenishment of consumables within the conference room (e.g. bottled water, glasses, mints etc.) and tidying of the tables prior to delegates returning. This can be regarded as 'preventative' action; far better to plan for this to happen as a matter of professional routine than to allow something to go wrong (e.g. the conference runs out of water) and have to expend inordinate effort putting it right. This can be called the 'egg on the fork' syndrome. If a restaurant is badly prepared and not checked, then there are things in there waiting to create maximum disruption – the eggy fork will be discovered by a guest, who will demand its replacement at the busiest point of service, causing widespread disruption. Typically there will be no spare forks in the sideboards, so the staff will have to go to the

wash-up to get one, a location where, mysteriously, there will also be no spare forks. This will necessitate the slowest washer-up in the entire building having to wash, dry and polish a fresh fork, taking the maximum possible time, while the guest's food, now cold, will have to be returned to the kitchen. Poor managers and lazy staff may regard good preparation as a nuisance, but it is, in fact, the bedrock on which all else is built. The same is true of clearing and cleaning. Cleaning equipment and materials must be available and accessible to the conferencing support staff. It may not always be a simple case of needing to clear up a broken glass. Delay in responding to these crises, major and minor, is typically due to lack of equipment, material and preparation.

Summary

The thoughtful and well-planned provision of catering services at conferences is essential to the high standard of the delegates' experience. Venues tend to be traditional in their menu planning, but this may be preferred, of course. Awareness of delegates' background needs to be shown. Clearly, the catering demands of the Chartered Institute of Accountants will vary considerably from that of the International Society of Epicures.

References

Cotterell, P. (1994) *Conferences: An Organiser's Guide*, Sevenoaks, Hodder and Stoughton, pp. 64–83.

Davis, B. and Stone, S. (1991) *Food and Beverage Management*, Oxford, Butterworth-Heinemann, 2nd edn, pp. 270–300.

Goldblatt, J.J. (1990) *Special Events. The Art and Science of Celebration*, New York, Van Nostrand Reinhold, pp. 107–117.

Kotas, R. and Jayawardena, C. (1994) *Profitable Food and Beverage Management*, Sevenoaks, Hodder and Stoughton, pp. 192–235.

Medlik, S. (1995) *The Business of Hotels*, Oxford, Butterworth-Heinemann, pp. 49–60, pp. 71–84.

Seekings, D. (1996) *How to Organise Effective Conferences and Meetings*, London, Kogan Page, 6th edn, pp. 94–96, 304–306, 333–335.

Warner, M. (1989) *Recreational Foodservice Management*, New York, Van Nostrand Reinhold, pp. 11–17.

Venison, P. (1983) *Managing Hotels*, Oxford, Butterworth-Heinemann, pp. 100–103.

7

Technical facilities _____

The aims of this chapter are:

1 To provide an overview of the type of technical facilities which are needed in conference venues:

- Basic presentation facilities
- Technical presentation facilities
- Backdrops and staging
- Lighting
- Sound

2 To consider the different technical facilities needed for a small conference and those required for a large one.
3 To discuss contemporary developments in facilities and the increasing level of sophistication of technology used at conference venues and available from production companies.

7.1   Introduction

The technical services that conference venues must provide are becoming increasingly sophisticated, to the extent that venue managers may choose to outsource the hi-tech needs of organizers and conference speakers to conference production companies. The larger and more important the conference, the greater the likelihood of the need for specialists, though a contributory difficulty is that venue managers may not be sufficiently knowledgeable of production companies and of what can be achieved with contemporary technology.

The set-up, or layout, of rooms may also impact on the technical facilities that can be used and how they will be prepared and located for a particular event. Various layouts are possible; common ones are shown in Figure 7.1.

In considering technical services, the small conference or meeting tends to retain relatively basic requirements. Where conferences have fewer than 30 delegates, unless the event is for VIPs, then the level of technology is typically fairly simple, little more complex than the provision of an overhead projector – yet even these can be adapted easily for use with computer generated text and graphics using portable liquid crystal displays (LCDs) and laptop computers. However, larger conferences are likely to need considerably more technical reinforcement.

Presentation methods certainly extend beyond the laptop-driven LCD display. Video projection of various kinds is available and is often used in conjunction with other media. 'Multimedia' can include video, computer generated text and graphics, transfer of pictures from digital cameras and the insertion of sound or video into presentations. Similarly, rapid development in communications has seen increasing use of video-conferencing and, at large-scale events, satellite links from one continent to another, enabling a presentation by a speaker in, say, Frankfurt, to be made at a conference on a video wall in Harrogate, though there is a significant difference between video-conferencing, which tends to be relatively small scale and interactive, and the latter.

In addition to the issues of visual or audio presentation and the means by which a speaker can illustrate or reinforce his/her work, there is also the issue of the image an organization may wish to foster among its delegates. In consequence, there has been a significant adoption of theatrical scene-building techniques to provide backdrops for conferences. This is not simply a matter of 'flats' (stage sets), the backdrop may need to include screens for video projection or 'gobo' projection (light projection) of logos; integration of video walls (even for the speaker who is actually on stage in the conference room itself, rather than far away) and of other specialist scenery, furniture and sound equipment may also be needed. Large-scale integrated staging and backdrops are mainly the province of production companies.

Beyond the visual presentation services, there are also the matters of lighting and sound. Lighting is of considerable concern, not only in terms of the creation of a suitable ambience and atmosphere for a conference (sometimes in rooms ill-adapted to the purpose) but also

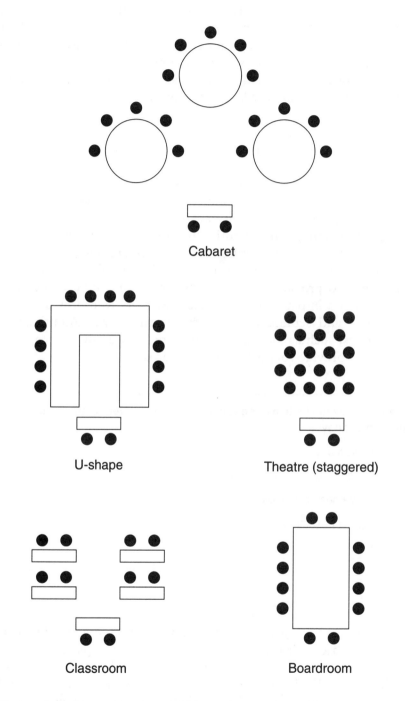

Figure 7.1   Examples of various room layouts used at conference venues (with or without specialist technical equipment)

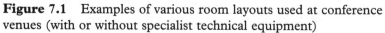

in terms of safety and security. The other technical issue is that of sound and the need for sound reinforcement in all but the smallest conferences. Sound reinforcement is provided by the use of microphones, amplifiers and loudspeakers. Some of the technicalities of these are considered together with the need for communication between technicians at very large-scale events.

7.2　Basic presentation

The vast majority of meetings and conferences, we have noted in earlier chapters, are relatively small. Most conferences have 30 or fewer delegates and 75 per cent have fewer than 100 delegates. For these small meetings, the essential 'technical services', as shown in Figure 7.2, may be fairly limited but still remain adequate for the job. All these items, such as overhead projectors (OHPs), are relatively cheap to provide and are portable; indeed some conference organizers, and in particular lecturers/presenters who provide training services and seminars, often provide their own. Additionally, some venues, such as management training centres and educational venues, will provide rooms with whiteboards.

There are five basic items of equipment that every venue, however small, must have:

- Flipcharts
- Video players and monitors
- Overhead projectors
- Slide projectors
- Screens

Figure 7.2

Speakers may use a variety of methods of presentation, but it is common to use overhead projectors for small groups, either with acetate film or to project LCD units. Colour laser printing also permits the production of high quality acetate materials at home and in the office. Computer software elements such as 'Clipart' also allow the incorporation of basic pictures into acetate slide design, enabling a relatively high quality product to be developed fairly simply and quickly. For slide projection 35 mm slides are required. While anyone can photograph suitable subject material on a good quality camera and illustrate a presentation easily, it may also be necessary to provide slides with graphics or charts which have to be provided by specialists. Most large towns have firms capable of doing this, both relatively cheaply and, with a reasonable amount of notice (normally at least one week), to a high standard. A little technical skill and careful preparation can provide a slide presentation of considerable effectiveness, if necessary with a taped commentary or using more than one slide projector.

For video use it is possible to buy a wide range of video cassettes, on a huge range of subjects. For management meetings there are two main 'ready made' sources. These are television programmes sold by the television companies or purpose-produced 'Management' videos, produced by video companies in fields such as general management, marketing, training, social skills etc. Videos of this type are somewhat expensive but usually worth the cost if being used for more than one presentation. Alternatively, it is possible to produce videos for a specialist purpose, but this would normally require a video company, though some universities and a few of the larger colleges may have the equipment and skills. But putting together a video for training use is not like making one of your neighbour's wedding. There is the question of what is needed in terms of objectives, then a structure, a script and the provision of adequate material (up to ten times the finally edited material may not be included because of poor quality and anything from bad light to heavy traffic noise). Material provided by amateur video makers often has poor production values, e.g. one camera in one place taking one view. This means there can be little or no intercutting or useful editing and views become extremely boring. In terms of the soundtrack there are issues of copyright (for music) and again of production values for narration – what do your narrators sound like on tape? Have you sound tested them? Finally, having collected a large amount of visuals and identified suitable sound, the whole has to be edited. Even if the material and recording can be done by well-read amateurs, the editing is likely to need someone with experience of the job in order to provide a good finished standard. Editing is also very time consuming – even a relatively simple 15-minute video may require up to two days of editing to achieve the desired standard.

7.3   Technical presentation facilities

The development of the technology to present information to an audience has moved extremely rapidly, from the point at which, 20 years ago, the highest level of technology would have been a 16 mm film projector of the kind used to project cinema films to a whole range of presentation methods ranging from the overhead projector to the video wall. While even the former, used commonly throughout conference venues, is capable of being adapted to a relatively hi-tech format, a far higher standard of presentation is achievable using a combination of projector and computer generated graphics. This is generally done using an LCD display which fits on top of the overhead projector, however, high powered projectors are required, of the order of two kilowatts (most projectors are generally only 650 watts). Speakers may bring their own equipment of this kind comprising an LCD display and a laptop computer to drive it, the presentation itself having been prepared on disc beforehand using appropriate software, such as 'Windows', 'Powerpoint' and 'Clipart'. However, some speakers will request the venue to provide equipment, wishing to bring only their own disc (Seekings, 1996).

In the field of video projection, similar techniques can be used; having developed the material, the speaker can use laptops (or PCs) to drive video projection. This can be done in a relatively simple format, rather like having prepared a set of 35 mm slides for use in a slide projector to illustrate a talk. The same 'bullet point' approach can be made using computer-driven video projectors, provided the appropriate software is available. More technologically advanced methods can be used in the preparation of multimedia presentations where text slides, video material and sound can be incorporated. If venues have suitable video projection available, the venue management and technical staff should request that speakers come and test (or send a copy disc of) their material at least a week prior to the conference. Not all systems are compatible and minor glitches such as cabling problems or insufficient attention to projected text size are as much a problem as compatibility (or lack of compatibility) of the equipment and software itself. It is unreasonable to expect that hi-tech presentations will work first time unless the speaker and venue are regular partners. In addition, the level of technical skill required to solve the simplest of equipment problems is not always available on the spot. While it is reasonable for a speaker to walk into a conference venue with a set of prepared OHP acetates and expect working projectors and adequate screens, the higher the level of technology or complexity the less the reliability, as a general rule.

Moving on from presentational issues, increasing sophistication of communications is also permitting advances in how, and where, conferences can be held. We have already noted the use of video walls for backdrops, but these are also used for the presentation itself and occasionally as part of a satellite link-up allowing a speaker in one location to address a conference in another. However, the resources required to do this may be limited, as few conference venues have satellite provision. The expense of provision still means it is generally cheaper to put the speaker on a plane and get him/her to the conference in person. On a smaller scale, video-conferencing is now extremely common, and video-conferencing rooms can be found in purpose-built conference centres, hotels, management training centres, large companies and educational venues. Video-conferencing tends to be smaller scale. The equipment at the affordable end of the market is chiefly intended for small business meetings between, say, two sites of a company, enabling meetings of up to 20 people to take place without half the people involved having physically to travel long distances to another site. Some conference venues provide video-conferencing rooms to enable organizations without the facilities to link up with those that have.

7.4   Backdrops and staging

Once a conference or meeting exceeds about 50 people, and for important events of less than that number, we begin to see a need for greater technical support. While technical support may be thought to be essentially aural or visual reinforcement (additional sound or lighting systems), it is increasingly the case that conference organizers (on behalf of both the corporate and the association markets) are looking for a standard of presentation which is extremely high, and are willing to pay for it. Considering this in a sequential way, the first element of conference technical support that delegates arriving in a conference hall are likely to encounter is the backdrop.

The days are long gone when presenters would be quite happy to stand up and make their presentation to a large audience using no technical support except a slide projector and a piece of car aerial as a pointer. Consequently the backdrop, or staging, is of major concern. It not only provides the location of a screen but is also the place where the corporate image is demonstrated (Goldblatt, 1990).

The backdrop may, of course, be simple; a contained screen with banner and a little special lighting. On the other hand, the backdrop may be a matter of considerable technical expertise incorporating stage design elements (Holt, 1993). These elements may range from the preparation and construction of stage flats (Thomas, 1991) to back projection and theatrical-style lighting. 'Gobos' are often used for backdrops; these project screen designs which can either be provided from a range of prepared formats, such as cityscapes, star fields etc., or, more commonly, be purpose-made with a logo or theme to use as a backdrop.

It is also more common for large-scale events to use video walls composed of a bank of TV monitors. This has been a feature of special events at concerts and gigs for some time, to enable very large (often outdoor) audiences to see the performers. They are used at large conferences both as a means of providing a backdrop and also to enable delegates in large conference halls to see the speaker and specialist material being presented. Such large-scale backdrops are generally constructed and set up by a production company which will deal with this type of highly technical presentation. The company may work regularly with a particular venue, as most of the large purpose-built venues have links with local production companies, but where this is not the case, or the production company is working at a new venue, it will have to undertake preparatory site work to assess factors such as available space, power, structural capacities and access to the hall or arena.

7.5   Lighting

The lighting of conference venues has a number of purposes. In terms of conference rooms themselves, the main purposes are to provide ambient lighting in the conference room enabling delegates to see, to provide highlighting of speakers and the lighting of backdrops. In the other areas of conference venues the lighting has to provide adequate background illumination in both public and support areas, and provide some decorative illumination, particularly in VIP rooms, dining areas and foyers. The final lighting issue is one of provision for safety, particularly in terms of exits and traffic routes with the building.

In conferences and meetings where the room layout or number of delegates requires it, or where there is staging and/or a backdrop of some kind, the lighting available must be suited to attract the attention of delegates to the speaker. This is likely to involve the use of direct lighting of the lectern, if one is in use, or the top table (wherever the presenter is speaking from). However, semi-darkness badly affects delegates' ability to concentrate and not only should a lectern area be illuminated directly, but the backdrop should have a good general diffused light. To this can be added some back lighting or indirect lighting to give atmosphere. Care must be taken, if a top table is in use (with several people besides the main speaker), that the lighting does not 'wash them out' or give them an odd colour (if, for example, blue washes are being used for the backdrop, this may have to be countered in the table areas so as not to make the people at the table also appear blue).

The conference room, in general, requires sufficient ambient lighting, usually of a diffused type, to permit delegates to take notes and to interact with other delegates. Not all conference rooms have natural light, and some are claustrophobic. A reasonable standard of lighting design with the careful use of diffused ceiling lighting and also some decorative lighting, wall lights and chandeliers perhaps, may serve to reverse the effect of a claustrophobic room (though lighting alone will not achieve this; good ventilation and air conditioning, even consideration of the plants used in a room, from the point of view of influencing the sense of smell, may also be needed).

Diffused illumination is also necessary in the public areas of a building. Corridors, toilets, foyers and reception areas should be well lit, though not harshly so. This is necessary to enable the proper functioning of these areas, to ensure safety and security, and to maintain a pleasant general ambience. Consideration must also be given to lighting control systems, dimmers and sensor switches. Typically the scalar illumination of public rooms should be of the order of 200 lux, with corridors and background areas having approximately 100 lux (Lawson, 1995). Areas where there is particular work taking place, such as reception area, kitchens, offices and so on, will require up to 400 lux.

Emergency lighting is necessary, and a legal requirement, in public buildings. Typically this is provided by secondary battery-powered light lasting up to two hours, activated by the fire alarm system or a power failure. Exits should be clearly illuminated and the emergency lighting adequate to allow escape. In some modern buildings, floor lighting strips are provided along exit routes, similar to those provided in aircraft floors to direct people to emergency exits. Security lighting is also necessary for areas containing expensive equipment, such as computers. Externally, particularly in car parks, and around the building, good lighting is needed to ensure delegates feel secure. Illumination of this kind also serves the general lighting purpose to deal with dark winter evenings.

Lastly, not so much an issue of being able to illuminate a room, but of being able to darken it, there is a need to provide functioning curtains or satisfactory blinds to enable presentations to be given in blackout where those presentations involve slide projection, video, LCD display or multimedia. This is often inadequately done, with some venues spending large amounts of money on highly sophisticated projection equipment, but failing to invest a little in providing a good blackout, let alone automated curtain-drawing systems which may be necessary in large rooms and where the first attempt to draw the curtains often results in the curtain jamming or detaching itself from the track.

7.6   Sound

Conferences exceeding 30 delegates will require sound reinforcement or put more simply, a sound system. Historically, the 'sound system' in conference venues was, at best, a microphone and a couple of loudspeakers, and if you were lucky, an amplifier, mixer and a deck for some recorded music. This is inadequate for contemporary needs, and while some speakers resist advice to use a microphone, thinking that their voice will carry through a large room with over 100 people in it, hecklers from the back (who cannot hear the speech) will usually disabuse them of this fallacy. The provision of sound systems is very necessary. Not only is there the simple issue of presenters and moderators being able to address the proceedings, there is also the issue of the need for sound reinforcement to go with visual tools, video and multimedia presentations. The small speaker built into the video monitor or projector is generally inadequate in a room with more than a few people in it.

Sound systems comprise microphones for the spoken word, amplifiers, mixers, loudspeakers and a variety of sound sources for music and other projected sound. Notwithstanding copyright law, music may be taken from cassette or CD, the latter being of a generally higher standard. Despite this, only a few major venues are adequately equipped to provide CD-based sound; while almost every home in the country has a CD player, not enough hotels or municipal venues are so equipped. Conference organizers wishing to incorporate good quality sound often have to hire in the necessary equipment to provide it. Companies providing conference equipment and a number of conference production companies are able to provide equipment packages which will include not only public address (PA) sound systems but also projection systems and lighting. Given the complexity of these things, a package, including the hire of a technician (again an element few hotel venues may be able to provide), is often necessary.

The basic sound system comprises microphone, amplifier and loudspeakers. There are two main types of microphone commonly used at conferences by the presenters: lead mikes (attached to a wire) and radio mikes (which have a transmitter). Lead mikes are generally used if speakers are presenting from a static position such as a lectern; radio mikes are used if the speaker is to move around or does not wish to have to carry a lead mike (though some types of radio mike are hand-held, the usual method is to attach to the lapel of the speaker a small mike which has a separate belt-hung transmitter). The general positioning of the microphone has to be behind the loudspeakers to prevent feedback noise.

The amplifier reinforces the sound and transmits it to the loudspeaker, usually coupled to a mixer. The function of the mixer is both to allow technical adjustment of the sound and to enable sound from various sources to be used. So, for example, a conference with a top table may have both lead mike and radio mike in use plus sound from a video projection and background music, while delegates arrive and depart. The mixer allows these to be used and adjusted, and can also permit the use of one or more banks of loudspeakers, depending on the size of the room. Where a technician is needed to operate the mixer, the system will usually be placed at the back of a room so the technician can hear the product of his or her endeavours. In purpose-built venues there may also be separate facilities for technical support designed into the room in the form of a projection box at the back.

The loudspeaker system may, in some cases, be built into a room, but is often in the form of often quite large portable loudspeakers. These would normally be set up between presenters and audience, and would also normally be quite high up, at least above head height for a seated audience, to reduce the amount of sound absorbed by the audience. Most loudspeakers will be stand mounted, but in purpose-built venues can often be ceiling-hung from gantries designed for them. There are some issues of aesthetics to be borne in mind and increasingly loudspeakers are screened by some means such as lightweight curtaining, floral displays or careful illumination around them, so the loudspeakers themselves are in relative seclusion.

Where a conference is extremely large, and takes place in an arena-type venue, there may also be a need to allow communication between more than one technician. For this purpose it is preferable to provide a communication ring. While this can be done using 'walkie talkie' radios, there is a danger of these interfering with other systems; in consequence, the communications ring may well be a land line with headsets, comprising microphone and headphones to ensure that the technicians' communication is private. Sufficient time must be allowed for crews to set up extensive systems in the case of a large event. The complexity, not only of the sound system but also of projection and lighting rigs, often requires a high level of specialist knowledge and considerable time. This must be accounted for by venue management and conference organizers at the planning stage.

Summary

Technical facilities for the conference business have been increasing in complexity for some time. Although this may be considered a good thing, from the viewpoint of a presenter being able to make his or her presentation more interesting, the downside is that greater complexity may lead to greater possibility of technical failure, for a wide range of reasons. It is of considerable importance, therefore, that conference venues regard the fitting of new facilities both with seriousness and with a close regard for the reliability of the equipment being put in.

References

Clayton, K. (1986) *How to organize a better conference*, London, Hutchinson, pp. 71–72, 170–171.

Goldblatt, J.J. (1990) *Special Events*, New York, Van Nostrand Reinhold, pp. 65–68, 73–77.

Holt, M. (1993) *Stage design and properties*, London, Phaidon, pp. 36–51.

Lawson, F. (1995) *Hotels and Resorts*, Oxford, Butterworth-Heinemann, pp. 295–298.

Seekings, D. (1996) *How to Organize Effective Conferences and Meetings*, London, Kogan Page, 6th edn, pp. 135–207.

Thomas, T. (1991) *Create your own stage sets*, London, A&C Black, pp. 54–87.

8

Registration and support activities

The aim of this chapter is:

To provide an overview of the operational support activities which take place immediately prior to, and during, a conference.

- Correspondence checks and pre-con meetings
- The organizer's office
- Setting up and security
- Rehearsal
- Meeting room checks
- Welcome delegates
- During the conference
- Close down

8.1   Introduction

To a large extent the requirements for the conference 'on the day' are the business of the conference organizer. The venue may well have several events running at once, or in the case of hotels or educational establishments, the conference business will be only part of the activities taking place. This means that venue managers and floor managers tend to be involved in a supporting or 'troubleshooting' role, helping organizers to solve problems and ensuring facilities and services are available on time and as planned.

The arrangements of the conference itself, the speakers, the presentation, structure, chairing of meetings etc. are the organizer's business and not directly the subject of these readings (there are a great many books available on the general theme of 'How to organize' a conference from the point of view of the client or organization whose conference it is). The venue's chief concern is to ensure that everything expected materializes at the right time and in the right place, and therefore the details considered here, from checking the correspondence before the event to close down, should be seen from this viewpoint.

8.2   Correspondence checks and pre-con meetings

Having received the booking correspondence for a particular conference (which is generally the basis for a set of pre-arrival meetings, both internal and with the organizer), the conference sales co-ordinator or floor manager would need to review the details of the event, prepare the function list (see Chapter 11 for the full planning process), contact the conference organizer to check everything is in order and then normally expect the arrival of the organizer early on the day of the conference (or in the case of large events, possibly before, particularly if staging or complex setting up is required). These checks of arrangements between co-ordinator and organizer are made to deal with any final requests or changes to the booked details. This is to be encouraged, as a pre-con meeting between the venue and the organizer will often iron out any last-minute problems. Experienced conference organizers can be expected to phone or call in, up to a week beforehand or the day before, in order to make general checks, without any need for prompting by venue staff.

8.3   The organizer's office

In order to reduce stress on organizers and ensure there is a central point of enquiry for a conference, an organizer's office should be provided whenever a conference is going to be large, long running or VIP in nature. Where possible, offices should be in a convenient location (preferably not a hotel bedroom) and provided, as a minimum, with a phone/fax machine. Without this the venue itself will become the clearing house for any activity relating to the conference: the arrival of the staging, lighting and PA equipment, suppliers and speakers with queries, the organizer's chief executive wanting somewhere for a 'quiet meeting' before the conference, etc.

Providing another room is not a matter of politeness but one of considerable importance, without this, the venue staff at a large event will be inundated with enquiries with which they may not be able to deal directly, or find the organizer in time to deal with them.

8.4   Setting up and security

The most likely thing to arrive after the organizer at a large event is the backdrop (though some may take several days to construct and this should be foreseen in the scheduling and booking of the conference hall). A ground plan should have been made by the organizer and a copy left with the venue, to enable work to proceed if the organizer is not yet present or has been held up. The set will be followed by the technical equipment, lighting, sound rig and so on. At this point, once all the equipment is in place, cleaning can be done, the room laid out, message boards put up, and signing and other support activities such as the arrangements for the delegates check-in made.

Certain types of conference will involve security issues. For VIP or political events a security check may take place at some point prior to the conference starting, usually between set-up and delegates' arrival (in these cases the set-up will have to be completed at least a day prior to the conference). Police or Home Office security may physically want to check the conference room and may well use sniffer dogs and metal detectors to do so. In some cases delegates may be required to pass through metal detectors of the kind found at airports, with specialist security staff on duty, video surveillance and security checks of staff. At this level it is also likely that staff may be required to hold special passes, though it is common for all staff to be badged in some way, not only for the purpose of courtesy to the delegates, guests and visitors but as a routine security issue.

8.5   Rehearsal

Prior to any security checks, there may be a rehearsal of the technical facilities, particularly of sound and presentation systems. While this rehearsal may be a purely technical activity, for certain types of high profile conferences, product launches or public relations events, it is likely that the rehearsal may be of the 'full dress' kind including practice by the speakers, timing arrangements, acoustics and so on. Ushers, if required, can be briefed at this point, together with any meeters/greeters the organizer may have arranged. Briefings for casual and specialist staff should include elementary issues such as the location of toilets, cloakrooms, organizer's office, refreshment areas, delegates' check-in and what to do with the VIPs (such as direct them to a VIP hospitality room) prior to the start, and what action is required in an emergency, including the nature of the alarm system, emergency exits, assembly points, location of the medical centre if there is one, or how to get a first aider quickly if there is not (Maitland, 1996).

8.6   Meeting-room checks

Floor managers are responsible for the smooth running of the conference on the day. As part of this process, not only will the floor manager have met the organizer on arrival, but he or she will also have carried out last-minute quality control activities; these will include ensuring that the meeting room is clean and correctly laid out, and that associated facilities such as toilets and the delegate reception area are clean and tidy. This is usually done with a checklist – sometimes referred to as the housekeeping or 'pre-flight' checklist, which covers everything from clarity of signing to the condition of the exterior of the building, because first impressions count.

8.7   Welcome delegates

A delegate reception area should be ready for use prior to the start time, even if, in the case of small informal conference, it amounts to no more than a table with delegate badges and agendas for people to pick up as they arrive. Commonly, however, the conference organizer would be on hand at least half an hour prior to the published time to deal with arrivals. At large conferences he/she would be supported by check-in staff, normally one for every 50 delegates, either provided by the organization itself or by the conference venue, to ensure delegates find the right conference and do not get mixed up with any other activities taking place (Seekings, 1996). A list of delegates expected, plus badges, should have been made up prior to the event, and where security is an issue, delegates must be politely required to wear their badges, though normally most delegates are happy to wear badges even at informal events; not all, at informal events, may wish to and should not be compelled if they do not. But it is important that delegates are checked against the delegate list as this will provide accurate final numbers of the people attending and can be passed to catering staff for any last-minute amendments to be made to seating or refreshment arrangements. It is also the point at which, if necessary, special dietary requirements can be checked. It is also common at delegate check-in to issue information packs about the conference, including agendas, conference papers, delegate lists and a little information about the venue for delegates to take away with them. This latter should be provided by the venue's marketing department to the organizer, if the organizer is making up his/her own packs, to ensure that a selling opportunity for the venue is not missed.

For convenience of organization, where there are a large number of delegates, the registration process may split delegates alphabetically between two or more tables. It may also be necessary to provide either greeters or an information desk, or both, as queries by incoming delegates can slow down the check-in process. Queries can be dealt with by a greeter, or the delegates may be directed from registration to information desks. For convenience of issue, packs, badges and tickets (such as refreshment tickets) should be laid out in alphabetical order to ensure delegates are checked in speedily. It is preferable that this layout process should actually take the form of all items (badges, tickets and pack) being put into large envelopes and the envelopes stacked in a box; not only does this increase the speed but also saves a great deal of stretching over a vast array of material spread on a table. The envelopes can also be used for incoming messages for delegates (urgent messages can be highlighted on the conference room screens during refreshment breaks). The greeters have the additional function of helping direct delegates; while signage is necessary and important, people arriving in unfamiliar locations will look first for someone to ask, and look only secondly for (inanimate) direction signs.

8.8   During the conference

Conference sales co-ordinators and floor managers will, as a general rule, be able to leave organizers, speakers and delegates to get on with it once registration is complete and the conference proper has started. The floor manager and his/her staff become involved once again, chiefly, at refreshment breaks. Not only are these the points at which delegates get some relief from the conference proper, but also opportunities for the venue to undertake routine checks of the conference room, strip out and replace dirty glasses, refill water jugs, reclaim crockery, replace ash trays (if smoking is permitted, which is rarely) and deal with any spot cleaning needs. The chief problem with conference breaks is a lack of communication between organizers and floor managers. It is important to encourage organizers to pop out or call the floor manager if a session is running late, so catering staff can be informed. Organizers also have a tendency not to allow sufficient time for moving large numbers of delegates. If a session overruns it is easy to say 'we will cut lunch by 15 minutes' only to find that in practice it is difficult to do so, as delegates tend to move at their own pace, and organizers do not understand the length of time involved in service.

8.9   Close down

If there is an element of conference organization which is neglected by venues it is the close down. Some effort should be made to ensure all went well. Conference co-ordinators should be around to speak to organizers and delegates on departure to obtain verbal feedback and pick up comments. Comments need noting as part of a quality control cycle, and can be recorded as part of the 'conference history' to be referred to if the conference is a recurring event. Even relatively simple issues such as the chairman preferring a lapel microphone, or delegates wishing to have the curtains drawn, while not being perceived as being significant in terms of the huge number of events a venue undertakes each year, are significant issues to that conference and potentially important in ensuring repeat business, so must be regarded with due weight. Again, there is also a sales issue; one or more delegates may be interested in the venue and while they would not normally step out of their way to obtain information, can be asked for their business card and have information despatched to them if they are interested. A sales opportunity is a sales opportunity, personal contact being far more effective than advertising.

Clearing up follows to ensure the room is stripped, cleaned and tidied for the next event. It is helpful to encourage organizers to check the room, with the floor manager, to ensure removal of equipment, identify any damage and tie up any outstanding issues. Some organizers may also wish to take the invoice with them at this point, if the event was not pre-paid or was deposit covered; though equally some organizers will simply wish it sent on. The final stage in this

---

SHORELINE CONFERENCE CENTRE

Shoreline Conference Centre: Marine Parade East, Fiction on Sea, Essex CO00 0OO
Phone: 00000 718309 Fax: 00000 718388

Mr James Davies,
Hon. Secretary
East Anglian Windsurfers Association,
2 Coombe Lane,
Copdock,
Ipswich,
Suffolk, IP3 6FX   *18th May 1998*

Dear James,

It was a great pleasure to host the Windsurfers Association annual conference, here at Shoreline, once again this year.

As ever, I welcome your comments on your experience, the centre and the service you and your delegates received. I would be most grateful if you could spare a few minutes to fill in and return this questionnaire, now you have had a day or two to reflect. Any comments or observations are treated in confidence, but are very useful to us in ensuring the standard of service is as you would expect.

I look forward to providing the facilities and services of the Shoreline Centre for yourself and the Association again next year. Please let me know if you wish to make a provisional booking for then.

Yours sincerely

Rob Johnson
Guest Services Manager

Conference Standards: Guests: East Anglian Windsurfers Association

	☺	☺	☹
Handling of your booking	☐	☐	☐
Co-ordination	☐	☐	☐
Meeting-room arrangements	☐	☐	☐
Delegates receival	☐	☐	☐
Food quality	☐	☐	☐
Food service	☐	☐	☐
Staff attitude	☐	☐	☐
Attention of management	☐	☐	☐

Any general comments _____

Figure 8.1   Example of a feedback questionnaire

cycle may be to send out the venue's questionnaire, after a week or so, not only to obtain feedback but also to enquire if the conference will be repeated; some organizers may re-book immediately (Kotas and Jayawardena, 1994). Returned questionnaires should be discussed at venue management meetings to pick up any serious issues and add to conference histories (see Figure 8.1).

Summary

This chapter has provided an overview of the chief support activities which surround the delegates' arrival and check-in at a conference. It is extremely important that this process is handled smoothly as first impressions of the efficiency, or otherwise, of the venue, count for a great deal. The floor manager or sales co-ordinator should also be around towards the end of the event to encourage a friendly departure and as an opportunity for feedback or discussion with the organizer.

References

Daily Telegraph (1986) *How to Set Up and Run Conferences and Meetings*, London, Telegraph Publications, pp. 95–111.

Kotas, R. and Jayawardena, C. (1994) *Profitable Food and Beverage Management*, Sevenoaks, Hodder and Stoughton, pp. 215–220.

Maitland, I. (1996) *How to Organise a Conference*, Aldershot, Gower, pp. 195–202.

Montgomery, R.J. and Strick, S.K. (1995) *Meetings, Conventions and Expositions*, New York, Van Nostrand Reinhold, pp. 184–189.

Rutherford, D.G. and Umbreit, W.T. (1993) Inproving interaction between meeting planners and hotel employees. *Cornell Hotel and Restaurant Quarterly*, **34**(1), February, pp. 68–80.

Seekings, D. (1996) *How to Organise Effective Conferences and Meetings*, London, Kogan Page, pp. 320–341.

Part Three _____

Management Issues _____

9

The Organization and staffing of conference venues

The aims of this chapter are:

1 To examine the organization of staff and the determinants of staffing level in conference venues.
2 To consider the role of staffing as a component of the conference product.
3 To identify the major determinants of staff levels within a conference venue.
4 To review the need for training and education of staff at operational and managerial level, within the context of assuring adequate service standards.

9.1   Introduction

One of the themes which has emerged in the preceding readings is that of the diversity of the conference business in terms of its component sectors, anything from hotels to educational establishments. The organizational issues mirror this diversity. It is extremely unlikely that any two conference venues would have exactly the same organization structure or staffing levels. This said, there are many similarities and we would expect all conference venues to provide core services which would be organized in a broadly similar way. There is some likelihood, therefore, that conference venues would be provided with organizational structures which cover perhaps five main functions: conference operations; hospitality and facilities management; marketing and sales; personnel and training; finance and control.

These five functions can be further subdivided depending on the nature of the relevant conference venue, but were we to survey the organization charts of a large sample of venues, all five functions would probably be present in some form. Staffing is, in part, determined by the organization structure, but it is also determined by a range of other factors as well; these are identified in Figure 9.1.

- The size of venue

- The ownership

- The age and design of the buildings

- The method by which the services are provided

- The levels of demand

Figure 9.1   Determinants of staffing

As with many other labour-intensive service industries, the conference business has a considerable need for trained staff. This need is satisfied by both on-the-job training and by the recruitment of staff from outside, whether direct from the labour pool or by recruiting from colleges and universities. Unlike other service industries, however, there are very few conference-specific courses in the UK and none in Ireland (though conference modules often exist on hospitality related higher education courses), which means that the conference business has to rely very heavily on adapting its staff from other sources such as the hospitality or tourism industries and from colleges where courses are taught in these fields.

9.2   Organization

The organizational framework of a conference centre forms the structure within which the various activities and services are provided. It has been previously noted that conference centres or venues provide four elements of the product: conference rooms and meeting services; food and drink services; presentation and technical services; support and ancillary services. In addition to these elements, a conference venue will typically have a sales department whose role may cover not only sales *per se*, but also conference planning and co-ordination, depending on the type of operation. There is also likely to be an accounts and control function, to deal with both outgoing and incoming invoices and financial business, and which may also include a purchasing role, particularly in larger venues. Underpinning the support activities, almost all venues will have a maintenance or facilities department of some kind, this may be a relatively closely confined activity, dealing just with the upkeep of the premises, or it may be much wider, taking in the field of facilities management and possibly covering not only premises and housekeeping, but any role not directly related to the core activity of selling meeting space. In some cases the facilities management role is referred to as 'hotel services' and covers everything from meeting-room cleaning to catering and upkeep of the building.

The organization of conference venues into respective departments, or operating areas, varies considerably from establishment to establishment and no two will be alike. It is possible, however, to generalize, and to look at the management structure of venues highlighting both similarities and differences. Taking hotel-based conference facilities, the level of complexity and interaction between the hotel core function of providing accommodation, food and drink, on the one hand, and providing conference facilities on the other, leads to considerable overlap. All parts of the organization report to a general manager, with various departments being more or less concerned with conference-related activities. Hotels have departments responsible for conferences under a 'conference and banqueting manager', whose department is probably split into conference and banqueting sales and conference and banqueting operations (Mullins, 1992; Lundberg, 1994).

Purpose-built conference centres, being self-contained, are structured rather differently. Given that purpose-built centres are often extremely large, perhaps capable of accommodating 2000 delegates or more, it might be expected that the number of staff is similarly large. This depends on whether all functions are carried out in-house or whether functions are outsourced, and to what extent. The organization chart of the National Exhibition Centre group gives us some indication of the roles that a large organization in this field requires – see Figure 9.2.

The organization chart of a typical conference centre, will, however, be somewhat different from the group organization of the NEC and will depend not only on the specific roles themselves, but also on the span of control within the organization and the levels of

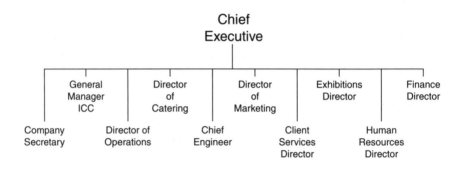

(*Source*: NEC, 1996)

Figure 9.2   Organization of the National Exhibition Centre Group

management, maintenance and other services which are outsourced or fall within the organization. Two more organization charts illustrate this, Figure 9.3 for a hotel conference and banqueting operation, and Figure 9.4 for a specialist conference venue. In the case of the latter chart, for a specialist conference venue, we are assuming all the services are undertaken in-house.

9.3   Staffing as a component of the conference product

The two principal issues of staffing as a component of the conference product are:

1 The provision of the conference product is impossible without staffing, and the conference product is in many respects service and labour intensive.
2 The quality of a given conference product is dependent, at least in part, upon the service standards that staff can achieve.

The nature of the conference business is such that each occasion is unique and a production line approach cannot be adopted. The activities undertaken to provide one meeting effectively may not necessarily accomplish the next so effectively, though there are clearly common features. Thus the recurrence of routine tends to be in the framework – the approach, the organization and the management of

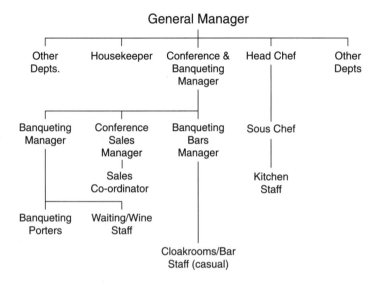

Figure 9.3 Example of a hotel conference and banqueting organization (the organization structure will vary from hotel to hotel)

conferences, rather than in the implementation or the operation. On a simple level, the same booking system can be used almost universally within one venue for all events, and a limited range of room layout styles can be used for most events; but the number of delegates, the timing, the speakers and their requirements will be unique for each event. It is this uniqueness that systems and staff must be sufficiently flexible to cope with.

Systems and staff are intended to work hand in hand. In general, to reduce costs, especially labour costs, if an operation can be systematized or automated it will be, but this supposes a more or less standard product. Nevertheless, many conference-related activities, such as food production can be, and are, systematized, whether this is via dish production to standard recipes and photographic specification of plated food layout, or the buying in of a standardized product from a supplier.

The maintenance of standards in non-routine service activities is a significant concern of management in a business such as confer-

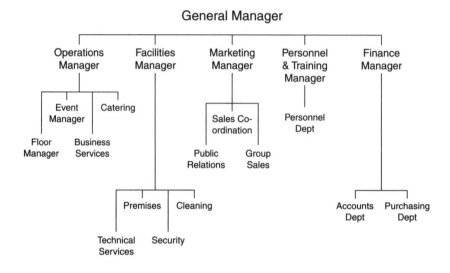

Figure 9.4   Example of a hotel conference and banqueting organization (the organization structure will vary from hotel to hotel). The above organization chart is really only indicative of the roles found within a conference venue; in reality organization charts are different in every organization and may represent anything from a closely adhered to hierarchical structure, to merely representing information flow from one sector to another. Normally, where a chart represents the hierarchy of authority, it will be accompanied by a range of job descriptions which deal with the responsibilities and role of each job.

encing. The non-routine and non-systematized nature of anything from room layout to variances in individual conference organizer requirements needs to be accommodated by allowing flexibility of operations while maintaining adequate supervision and control (Lovelock, 1994).

Simple managerial control may be exercised by detailed supervision and the use of checklists; by techniques such as 'management by exception'; or by improving the quality of staff and staff training to the level at which quality control can largely be placed in the hands of the staff themselves. The managerial strategy adopted varies from organization to organization and the effectiveness of the strategy is as much dependent on the ability of the managers themselves as the systems set up to achieve appropriate standards.

9.4   Determinants of staffing levels

Notwithstanding the comments already made about the effect of different types of organization on staffing levels (e.g. type of centre; in-house or outsourced) there are a number of other factors which affect the level of staffing, and in part the organization of staffing, within a conference venue.

The size of venue

The range of meeting rooms; their capacities; the scale, range and extent of principal services such as delegate reception, catering, business centre, security, technical support etc.; the scale, range and extent of ancillary services such as cloakrooms, retail outlets, public facilities, parking, maintenance and facilities operations. The extent to which economies of scale are achievable and operations overlap (in venues which are part of other activities such as hotels, academic venues, multi-purpose venues etc.). Large centres would tend to have a lower staff to delegate ratio than smaller ones – if all other factors were equal.

The ownership

Partly linked to the issue of whether a venue is 'stand alone' or integrated with another operation, and whether the venue is owned by the commercial/private sector or the public sector. The extent of staffing will vary. It is possible that fewer staff are directly employed in venues which are the responsibility of group head offices (departments such as finance or personnel may only exist at head office) and in the case of publicly run venues, where similar functions are provided centrally.

The age and design of the buildings

Modern conference venues, particularly the large purpose-built centres are designed with ease of staffing in mind. In consequence, service cores tend to be centralized so fewer staff can operate and supervise a larger number of rooms and activities. This centralization of services and concentration of design also reduces transit times for staff going from one part of the venue to another, with corridor layouts designed for speed and ease of access for both delegates and staff, rather than (in the days of assembly rooms) to allow two ladies to pass each other wearing crinolines and keep the servants separated from the guests!

The method by which conference services are provided

This is not chiefly an issue of the lay-up of meeting rooms and their servicing, it is more an issue of the provision of the principal services such as catering. The service of lunch to delegates may most easily be made by buffet or even self-service, therefore containing staffing levels to a bare minimum. (Of course, conference buyers and organizers are entirely free to specify higher levels of service, but this may be at an extra cost.) Related to the method of service is the issue of quality. A number of companies involved in the conference business seek to achieve a higher market share and differentiation of their venue by providing higher levels of service; to do this more (and probably better trained) staff will be needed. Staffing levels may also vary between venues because of differences in operating methods related to anything from shift coverage policy to the means by which food is supplied to the venue (e.g. fresh to be made up, pre-prepared to be re-heated; delivered complete requiring only service).

The demand for and scheduling of staff

Demand is a baseline determinant of staffing. In any venue, there will be a fixed level of staff beyond which it is not possible to fall (for example, a receptionist may be required to be on duty at any time between 7.00 a.m. and 11.00 p.m. seven days a week to deal with even a low level of business: visitors, general administration, enquiries by phone, fax, e-mail or whatever). The one receptionist may be able to deal with greater demand only up to a certain level (e.g. two 50-person conferences arriving with an hour of each other on the same day, but not being able to cope if both arrived at once). Thus, as demand increases so too will staffing, including not only full-time staff but also part-time and casual staff.

The control of the cost of staffing is also a major concern. Rosters are produced by management to schedule staff, yet cost control is as much dependent on effective forecasts of demand and careful rostering as it is on the sheer number of staff. A comparison of two managers compiling a roster for the same unit, the same demand forecast and the same staff could still produce a significant variance in cost due to the ability of each to complete an appropriate roster effectively. More efficient rostering could, perhaps, reduce the number of staff needed and is thus also a determinant, though not a major one (Medlik, 1995).

9.5   Training and education of staff

In order to achieve sufficiently high standards of service and management of conference operations it is necessary to employ people with adequate skills and to provide additional training. Historically, the acquisition of suitable staff for conference venues has been achieved by two main methods:

1 The employment of staff with a good basic education to be trained by the organization and developed as a skilled member of staff and/or as a manager.
2 The employment of staff with an appropriate vocational and educational background in the field or a related field.

The first method, effectively on-the-job training, is the most prevalent for operational staff. Staff, and managers, have been developed in-house by experience or by the venue providing some form of basic training. In the case of relatively unskilled jobs such as banqueting porters (the job in hotel venues of setting up and laying out meeting rooms), these have tended to be based on recruiting a person with satisfactory potential, and good social skills, who could learn the job by experience through working with other existing banqueting porters. This method is sometimes backed up by additional short-course training in addition to fundamental activities such as induction and fire training. It is still possible, therefore, for a member of staff to work his/her way up through an organization to supervisory or management level by experience over a period of time.

The second method, based on vocational education, provides not only operational staff but also supervisors and managers. Larger organizations recruit from colleges or universities which run appropriate courses and then tend to add their own programme of experience or experience linked to a company training course to develop managers with a specific knowledge of their company. Yet it must be noted that there are almost no conference industry-specific further or higher education courses in Britain or Ireland. In order to recruit, say, a junior conference sales co-ordinator, the most likely educational source would be vocational courses in the hospitality and catering field. These range (in the UK) from GNVQ programmes, through Higher National Diploma courses to undergraduate courses at degree level. Only at degree level do some colleges and universities include conference-related modules or, in a very few cases, conference-related pathways to their degrees. Other potential sources of vocationally educated people are the travel and tourism fields; sales and marketing, and business studies. Typically people employed from these fields, particularly the hospitality field, will have a good background knowledge of business generally and some awareness of conferencing as an activity, but will still need specific training, for two reasons:

- Every organization is different
- Every job is different

Even using graduates from those colleges and universities where the degree programme contains a specific conference element, a conference venue will need to tailor the graduates they have employed to their particular organization and role. Nevertheless there is a good level of co-operation between educational establishments and conference centres. These links range from industry co-operation with assignment work and field visits, up to providing year-long paid placements for undergraduate students. By this method the conference industry not only influences the curriculum content of courses, but also effectively provides 'seed corn' for future employment, among those students with an interest in conferences. A number of the companies providing year placements may well go on to employ some of the placement students once those students have completed their course. This system, which is particularly well established between conference venues and the greater hotel schools, is mutually beneficial and often seen as a model of good practice for other industries.

In addition to the above methods, the ebb and flow of employment in general accounts for a large number of staff and managers within the conference business – people moving jobs from one location to another, people moving into conferencing from related fields (e.g. hospitality, tourism, retail, business travel), people newly employed in their first job and staff being transferred around the larger, more diverse organizations which may include several divisions besides conference activities. All these methods account for the supply of potential staff, some are better trained than others, but in all cases there is a good business argument for organizations to have a well-trained, well-motivated and well-managed staff (Swarbrooke, 1995). This also is the reason for many organizations having a definite staff development policy, progression routes and comprehensive staff training programmes, some of which are targeted at quality issues such as programmes in 'Investors in people', which are intended to achieve not only high levels of staff training and good service for delegates, but also to achieve public recognition in general.

Summary

The organization of conference venues varies from place to place. While there may be some commonality of structure and job title within component sectors, such as hotels, the variation is still considerable. Staffing levels are determined by demand, and also by the size of venue and variants such as the service standard provided. The conference business relies heavily on staff from related fields, such as hotel management or tourism, to obtain both experienced people and college leavers with the right kind of potential.

References

English Tourist Board (1992) *The Handbook of Tourism and Leisure*, Cambridge, Hobsons, p. 24.

Lovelock, C.H. (1994) *Product Plus*, New York, McGraw-Hill, pp. 160–190.

Lundberg, D. (1994) *The Hotel and Restaurant Business*, New York, Van Nostrand Reinhold, pp. 119–129.

Medlik, S. (1995) *The Business of Hotels*, Oxford, Butterworth-Heinemann, pp. 71–93.

Mullins, L.J. (1992) *Hospitality Management – A Human Resources Approach*, London, Pitman, pp. 52–85.

National Exhibition Centre Group (1996) *Information pack for the International Conference Centre, Birmingham*, Birmingham, NEC Ltd (Unpublished), p. 5.

Swarbrooke, J. (1995) *The Development and Management of Visitor Attractions*, Oxford, Butterworth-Heinemann, pp. 226–242.

UCAS (1996) *Guide to University and College Courses 1997*, Cheltenham, Universities Central Admission Service.

10

Some issues in the marketing of conference venues

The aims of this chapter are:

1 To explore the demand generators for the conference business – corporate and association demand – in the context of the organizational buying process.
2 To consider some of the range of marketing techniques relevant to venues.
3 To explore the role of conference placement agencies in the conference buying process.
4 To consider some asset management issues related to the operation and marketing of conference venues.

10.1 Introduction

Historically, the conference buyer was one person who was both buyer and organizer. That person rang up a few venues, asked for a brochure, waited a few days, looked at the brochures and then went to visit a couple of venues before making a decision. This still happens, but as companies and conferences have grown bigger, it might not be one person; it might be a group or a committee that is the 'buyer' and therefore a conference centre might have to influence them all, not just one person, to get the business. Also, because of the size and complexity of conferences, the buyer may not want to organize it directly, but would rather just say, 'here is the budget' to someone else who organizes conferences professionally; thus there are now intermediaries in the conference business, ranging from professional organizers to placement agencies who will do some or all of the organizing. Clearly, this makes the role of the marketing department of a conference venue extremely important and increasingly complex.

On the other hand, many of the factors which determine a buyer's decision about where to hold a conference have not changed. It is still the case that the foremost issue about a choice of venue is location, closely followed by transport and access, and the quality of the venue.

There is a tendency, due to the lack of specialized education for conference venue managers, not to import management concepts, such as yield management, from other industries. As a consequence, this technique is discussed here, briefly, to illustrate its use in a conference venue context; therefore, the facility operations of conference venues are discussed. While meeting-room provision is the core activity of a conference venue, subsidiary or support activities such as catering, cleaning and premises operations may be outsourced. This is a major trend in property operation generally, but caution must be exercised, as with outsourcing goes the loss of direct control and this may negatively impact on delegates' views of the centre, if not handled properly.

10.2   The organizational buying process

In an earlier chapter, two major markets were identified – the corporate market and the association market; the latter was also further broken down into professional associations and voluntary associations (Davidson, 1994). Each of these markets varies in its buying process, i.e. who buys the conference within an organization. We must be careful, also, to differentiate between conference buyers and conference organizers, as the two may not be the same, nor may they even be within the same organization.

Conference buyers are the originators of the demand for the conference within an organization. This is more complex than it first appears, since a large organization, particularly in the corporate sector, may have more than one buyer: a large, multidivision international company may be organized in such a way that each division is responsible for its own conferences, or conversely, the company may have one person responsible for all conference buying. How an organization does this is of considerable importance to the sales managers of conference venues. Within the corporate sector, conference buyers may either go direct to conference venues to organize a conference or via an intermediary, such as a conference organizer, or a conference placement agency.

The association sector is rather different. Professional associations tend to have small centralized secretariats for a large number of members. The secretariat may (or may not) have enough expertise to handle regular conferences (the same is true of small corporate organizations) and again may use an intermediary. The secretariat is thus the buyer for the association. Voluntary associations are often even more loosely organized; a few have permanent paid secretariats or chief executives, but many consist of honorary officers or unpaid committee members. In such cases the buyer may be a whole committee or just one member.

For conference venues, the difficulties of marketing to a disparate and wide range of potential buyers, some through intermediaries, some not, is clearly evident. Additionally, the organization structures of many companies, and large associations, may result in the actual decision maker being hidden. (For example, let us suppose the buyer of a large multinational company is the UK training division. The buyer is the chief training manager within the division: He or she may actually be part of a committee responsible for organizing the annual conference, and while the chief training manager and the committee have supposedly got responsibility, in practice they have to report their choice of venue to the UK Divisional Director, who has the final say. In some organizations this type of reporting may be a simple rubber-stamping, in others the real power may lie with the Divisional Director.) Who then, must the conference venue target in its sales effort, and how? In practice, while the sales managers of conference venues are often simply being responsive to incoming enquiries or repeat business, where a venue wishes to tap a new market or capture a new organization's business, there is clearly a need to know who the buyer actually is. Figure 10.1 illustrates the variations in links between the venues and the buyers. Figure 10.1(a) and (b) illustrate a relatively simple approach to booking a conference, where both the process and the organizations involved are operating in a direct way. As organizations become larger, the process of booking and organizing a conference may become more complex and the need for specialist help in either placing the conference or undertaking the organization of it, also may become more complex, see Figure 10.1(c) and (d). Figure 10.1 (e) and (f) illustrate that, in large organizations, the decision-making process is often diffused and may involve a large number of people, not only in a committee perhaps, but also in the form of influencers and gatekeepers.

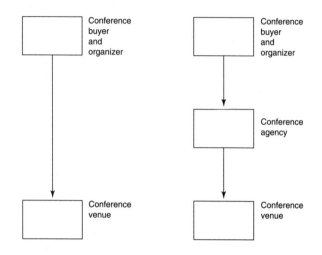

(a) An organization going direct to venue

(b) An organization using an agency

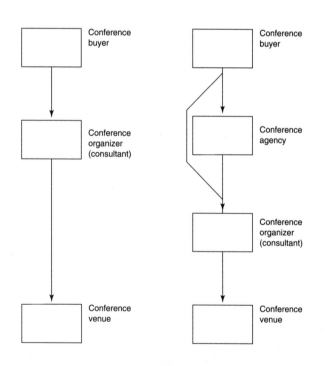

(c) An organization using a consultant

(d) An organization using an agency and a consultant

Figure 10.1   Conference buyers and intermediaries

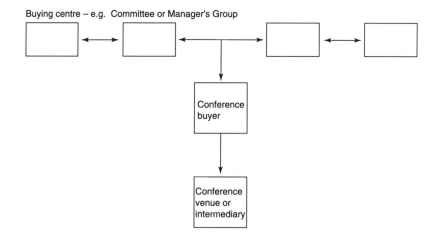

Buying centre – e.g. Committee or Manager's Group

Conference buyer

Conference venue or intermediary

(e) Committee in an organization with buying authority

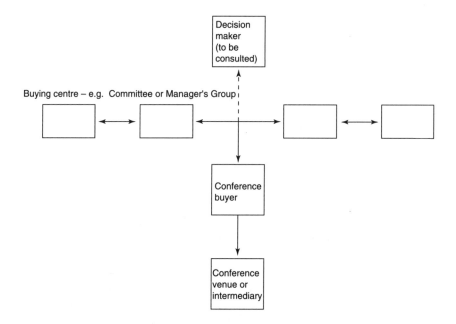

Decision maker (to be consulted)

Buying centre – e.g. Committee or Manager's Group

Conference buyer

Conference venue or intermediary

(f) Committee in an organization acting within the authority of someone else

Figure 10.1   Conference buyers and intermediaries (continued)

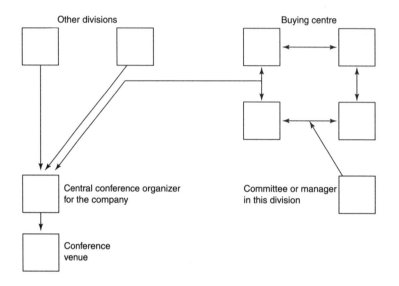

Other divisions

Buying centre

Central conference organizer
for the company

Committee or manager
in this division

Conference
venue

(g) Large multidivisional organization with an in-house organizer

Figure 10.1   Conference buyers and intermediaries (continued)

10.3   Determinants of the buying process

The determinants of the buying process can be seen in two ways –
those that are general to the sales process overall, and those that are
specific to a buyer. General determinants can be seen as being relevant to the sales and marketing of other activities and products, not
just conferences; see Figure 10.2 (Kotler et al.,1996).

A number of specific determinants can be seen as being conference business or conference buyer specific. If the conference is in the
hands of a conference organizer or conference placement agency,
these are the issues which are relevant to where the conference may
be held, see Figure 10.3. Of these, by far the most important is location, whose closeness to a motorway and the venue being within one
hour of a major city and an airport are major influencing reasons in
the buying process for conferences (Coopers and Lybrand Deloitte,
1990; Maitland, 1996; Seekings, 1996).

Determinants of the buying process in general include

- The buying cycle (decision times, lead times)
- Price sensitivity to the product (high cost, low cost, total package)
- Service sensitivity to the product (service quality)
- Opportunities for add-on sales ('up-selling')
- Buying pattern factors – geographic (international or national)
- One-off or repeat sales opportunities (annual, biannual, monthly)
- Product familiarity (buyer knowledge and awareness)

Figure 10.2

Determinants of the conference buying process include

- The location; distance to airports; closeness to motorways, etc.
- Standard of accommodation and of conference rooms
- Excellence (or otherwise) of staff
- Prices
- Range of conference rooms available
- Ability to handle large conferences
- Attractive surroundings
- Reputation of the venue

Figure 10.3

10.4   Marketing for new business

Marketing techniques employed by conference venues vary, but the range of approaches for sales managers is extremely wide. Nevertheless the nature of the conference buying decision and the influencing factors make targeting buyers relatively complicated. The venue managers' and venue sales teams' expertise in selling their conference centres may also not always be of a particularly high standard, perhaps tending to rely on general advertising and responses to incoming enquiries (Hartley and Witt, 1994), rather than, for example, personal sales calls.

The student of the conference business would probably automatically think of advertising as the major marketing tool available to conference centres – all you do is advertise in the right place and conferences come flocking to you. Would that it were so easy. Advertising has its place and plays a significant role in raising awareness and helping support an image for a venue. It is particularly relevant on a local scale for conferences organized by individuals in the corporate sector or by the voluntary association market, who do not have the time or the knowledge to examine other sources. Thus small conference hotels do advertise for local business and this may be a significant part of their effort. However, larger venues take a wider range of approaches, which may include not only advertising and public relations but also the use of 'advertorials' – pieces in trade magazines describing the venue in an attractive and narrative way, as well as a range of other marketing tools.

Important as advertising may be, an increasing proportion of the business is undertaken at conference or conference-related exhibitions. There are a number of these events during the year, many in London, some at other locations such as the National Exhibition Centre. These events include the 'Annual International Confex', which is currently the largest of these events, enabling significant numbers of buyers and sellers to get together under one roof. However, many similar fairs take place, including the Meetings and Incentive Travel Show; the British Association of Conference Destinations exhibition; and the Conference and Corporate Hospitality Show. Not only do these events provide a showcase for venues, but also for related organizations such as production companies and event management organizations. Most visitors to these exhibitions are potential buyers – corporate organizers, association organizers, agency representatives and other event organizers. Exhibitions of this kind are therefore, probably rightly, seen as an excellent way of generating business (Poorani, 1996).

Whereas the above events provide a marketing window for many venues, individual venues also attempt to entice buyers, organizers, agency staff and bureau staff by providing familiarization visits, a kind of incentive travel for the conference business. Buyers are invited to view the facilities and will be provided with information and hospitality in an effort to show off the advantages of the venue. In this way buyers not familiar with a centre can be influenced, or at least informed, of the facilities and services offered.

Public relations activities are also important, and while familiarization visits may well be significant for buyers, most conference venues are also prepared to put on general visits for members of the public, on a kind of 'open day' basis, once or twice a year, plus similar events for local business people as part of a more general approach. The final category in this field of activity is show-rounds for educational establishments, professional venues being aware of the fact that not only is there a community-image benefit of providing educational tours, but also that the students visiting may well be the sons and daughters of local business people or conference buyers. As such they may well be as much opinion formers as any other visiting group.

10.5   Marketing for repeat business

It is axiomatic in conference marketing that new business costs between eight and ten times more than repeat business to create. But, the nature of new business often presents a more exciting challenge to venue marketers and sales people than does the careful routine of recording, monitoring, and caring for existing business. Yet it is the attention to the detail of maintaining, and enhancing, existing business which is probably the acid test of the marketing department of a conference centre. The development of existing business both into repeat business and as a lead to other business (including new business) is crucial to success. Let us suppose that a conference centre hosts an Annual General Meeting for a voluntary association, and has done so for several years. Is this the only conference business this association does? Are there any contacts that can be developed among the people organizing the AGM or attending it? Some basic effort at research, such as asking for a copy of the registration list, containing, hopefully, not only names of delegates but also their organizations, should yield a number of leads to be explored and some potential contacts. It is also important to attempt to keep current organizers 'warm', i.e. call and talk to them occasionally and invite them to familiarization and hospitality events. This ensures the contacts are maintained. While there is some consistency of organization in the corporate and professional association market, this is not the case in the voluntary association market, where organizers and organizing committees may change annually.

A number of conference venues run loyalty clubs, rather like the business clubs run by hotels. These provide a means of rewarding regular clients for their continued use of a venue and also assist in keeping track of clients' views about their past events (e.g. clients may often feel freer to make an observation about some aspect of the facilites or service, in the more informal atmosphere of a club hospitality evening, than they might have done at the end of their last conference, when they were in a hurry to get home), and as a means of obtaining sales leads for future events and keeping client histories up to date.

10.6   Marketing of the conference destination

In addition to the issues of marketing a venue alone, it should not be forgotten that a useful synergy may exist by marketing several venues together; this is seen in the American approach of using visitor and convention bureaux (Lundberg, 1994). This synergy is exploited by organizations such as the British Universities Accommodation Consortium and the British Association of Conference Destinations. Joint marketing efforts have considerable advantages, not only of the extension of the individual marketing to a wider audience, but also where one venue alone in a destination cannot deal with a whole conference but the business could still be obtained by two or more. This also applies in particular to destinations with a purpose-built conference centre which requires the provision of residential accommodation from one or more local hotels. To deal with this, many major cities have visitor and convention bureaux, often part of the local or regional Tourist Information Service, which not only provide a clearing house (central point) for enquiries but also produce additional publicity material and co-ordinate efforts to encourage buyers to come to that particular location. In the UK this role is undertaken by the British Association of Conference Destinations, in Ireland by the Board Fáilte Convention Bureau and in Europe, by its counterpart, the European Federation of Conference Towns.

A number of other organizations are involved, directly or indirectly, in promoting conference venues. These include the Tourist Boards and other authorities which promote the UK and Ireland overseas. Bearing in mind, for example, that London has been among the top three destinations for international conferences for many years (Law, 1993a), the efforts of the various bodies are of great importance.

10.7   Priorities in venue marketing budgets

The largest single cost in terms of marketing budgets for conference centres is the staffing cost of the marketing or sales department itself;

almost all larger venues, purpose-built conference centres and large hotel conference venues have dedicated sales teams and sales co-ordinators. Even smaller hotels will probably have at least a banqueting manager. Universities and multi-purpose municipal venues have a conference co-ordinator attached to their residency or catering department. Above and beyond this basic cost, the sales departments' budgets tend to include a number of main items for promotional purposes as identified in Figure 10.4. It is difficult to ascertain the effectiveness of the various methods, but the importance of direct marketing in this ranking of priorities (Coopers and Lybrand, 1990) would suggest that personal contacts are significantly important to the process.

Conference venue sales budgets may include

   1 Printing: brochures, leaflets and conference packs

   2 Direct marketing: sales visits to organizers/buyers, etc.

   3 Advertorials: journal/magazine articles

   4 Hospitality: familiarization visits, open days, loyalty clubs

   5 Exhibitions: stands as the main conference market exhibitions, e.g. Confex

   6 Agency contacts and commission

   7 Paid advertising: newspapers, magazines, direct mail, etc.

Figure 10.4

For all its modern complexity the final sale still depends on one piece of the jigsaw – the buyer picking up the phone or walking in and making an enquiry. So 'picking up the phone' may mean faxing you or e-mailing you, but it is still down to someone showing an interest in the venue – after that it is up to the sales team to convert an enquiry into a confirmed booking.

10.8 The role of conference placement agencies

Conference placement agencies are playing an increasing role in the conference business. Agencies save companies the time and effort of researching and booking a venue. Clearly, for a large national or multinational company, this is a significant advantage, as it means that companies do not have to employ in-house specialists.

Agencies operate by charging the client a commission of between 8 and 10 per cent of the value of a conference, and obtain their business by advertising, attending exhibitions for secretarial and managerial staff, making sales calls and tendering. In the latter case a national company may ask for tenders from agencies who wish to handle that company's conference business and will then award a tender, usually on a non-mandatory basis. What this means is that the agency in effect becomes a recommended, but not a mandatory, supplier. The agency then will have to promote its conference service to the different offices of the company individually; it may do so, for example, by visiting divisional or regional offices and meeting secretarial staff or by putting up a stand in the regional office for a day or two to ensure everyone is familiar with the service offered.

In this way, enquiries for potential conferences are received by the agency and are then processed by placing the conference at a suitable venue. Some agencies also operate a conference and events organizing arm, in order to deal with the whole conference package, not just the initial venue finding and booking process. Venues themselves encourage this placement activity by inviting agency staff to see their venues and also by offering 'override commission' to attract conference business.

10.9   Asset management

Regardless of the type of venue being managed and marketed, the investment in it is probably considerable. Even a basic meeting room requires space, furnishings, fixtures, fittings, services and equipment. A meeting room is therefore as much an asset to be managed as is any other space, be it a guest bedroom in a hotel or a seat on an aeroplane. In order for the asset to be of value and to generate wealth, it must be used to the maximum possible extent. The reader should note the careful use of the word 'wealth'. In many organizations this is replaced by the shorthand 'profit', which, strictly speaking, it is not. A meeting room may indeed generate a profit, but the generation of wealth is a wider concept, taking in not only profit (if appropriate to the organization) but also employment, the provision of a service, the contribution it makes to the community (via its use, payment of taxes towards community services, bringing delegates to the community etc.) and a range of other benefits from the provision of a dividend to shareholders even to a contribution to the built land-scape.

Managing the asset therefore comprises a network of sometimes conflicting activities and objectives. The reason for the focus of com-mercial organizations on profitability is the perception that the other objectives may not be fulfilled unless the asset is working sufficiently hard to make a profit. Much the same applies to conference facilities, with the proviso that not all organizations are profit making (e.g. charities and their use of stately homes as conference venues which may be, nevertheless, intended to contribute to the costs of an oper-ation).

The profitability of conference centres is sometimes questionable. Even the ICC, often quoted here, did not initially have an auspicious record of large profits (*Birmingham Evening Mail*, 10 February 1994). Supporters would agree this is because it is part of a greater strategy (i.e. urban regeneration) rather than as a large profit gener-ator *per se*, and also that there is a considerable lead time in a centre building up sufficient business from its opening date (Law, 1993a). Such arguments may be received cautiously as the research available into this and related industries suggests further work is needed to assess impact (Law, 1993b; Smyth, 1994).

Revenue generation in the conference business is based on the use of the meeting-room space and selling of subsidiary services such as catering. In order for this to be achieved it is necessary to utilize the space to its maximum possible extent at the highest possible tariff (consistently over time). This is the activity of yield management (Ingold and Bradley, 1993; Jauncey, et al., 1993). It should not simply be seen, however, as a manipulation of the space inventory and price range. A thorough awareness of the market segments using the conference centre is needed, together with their price sensitivity and revenue generating potential. This latter should be taken in the context of knowledge of costs per market segment. It is not enough simply to consider the various market segments alone (be these incentive conferences, small executive meetings, trade meetings or whatever).

It will be necessary to have comprehensive information available on the users of the centre, including historical demand patterns, a prediction of possible future demand and the actual demand as it occurs (from which variances can be identified). Some conferences are regular, e.g. monthly or yearly, or irregular. Having identified patterns, for occupancy purposes, the price each segment pays must also be considered. It is not enough to consider price solely on the

basis of room hire revenue, it is also a question of revenue generation to all other areas and over comparable periods, in relation to
costs. Thus it may be that a two-day residential conference for organization A may appear to be more profitable, based on the tariff
charged, than two separate single-day non-residential conferences
for organization B; but once other factors are applied, including cost
of operation, is this genuinely so?

Despite the potential for the analysis and exploration of high
volume, high revenue, low cost segments of the market, which yield
management may provide, the detail and effort needed to make
genuine like-for-like comparisons is significant. Indeed a number of
organizations involved in the hospitality and conference business
employ 'yield managers' just for this purpose. It must also be clear
that emphasis on the technique alone is not enough – yield management does not generate new business, it is an analytical tool. The
selling of the conference centre and the maintenance of the market
share in a competitive field, is as much an issue, if not more so.

Summary

There are a number of unique issues in the marketing of conferences. Of these, probably the most significant is that the client is very
often not a single individual. The client may be part of a larger organization, or may be one of a group, or may be a group of people
within an organization. This makes marketing conferences rather
more complex than marketing cans of beans. Even in what appears
to be a relatively simple decision-making process, the venue may
have to market its services to groups of people who influence the
decision makers and increasingly the marketing effort must also
extend to a range of intermediaries, such as placement agencies. In
addition to the widely understood issues of marketing, conference
centres also need to seek out further techniques, such as yield management, which can be applied to the business.

References

Astroff, M.T. and Abbey, J.R. (1991) *Convention Sales and Services*,
    New Jersey, USA, Waterbury Press, pp. 53–116.
Birmingham Evening Mail (1994) *City set to lose £7.2m on Centre*.
    Birmingham Evening Mail, 10 February, p. 10.

Coopers and Lybrand Deloitte (1990) *UK Conference Market Survey 1990*, London, Coopers and Lybrand Deloitte Tourism and Leisure Consultancy Services, pp. 13–20.

Davidson, R. (1994) *Business Travel*, London, Pitman, pp. 31–49.

Hartley, J.S. and Witt, S.F. (1994) Increasing the conversion rate of conference and function enquiries into sales. *International Journal of Hospitality Management*, **13**(3), pp. 275–285.

Ingold, A. and Bradley, A. (1993) An Investigation of Yield Management in Birmingham Hotels. *International Journal of Contemporary Hospitality Management*, **5**(2), pp. 13–16.

Jauncey, S. et al. (1993) The meaning and management of yield in hotels. *International Journal of Contemporary Hospitality Management*, **7**(4), pp. 23–26.

Kotler, P., Bowen, J. and Makins, J. (1996) *Marketing for Hospitality and Tourism*, London, Prentice Hall, pp. 217–236.

Law, C.M. (1993) *Urban Tourism*, London, Mansell, (a) p. 47, (b) pp. 154–65.

Lundberg, D.E. (1994) *The Hotel and Restaurant Business*, London, Van Nostrand Reinhold, p. 52.

Maitland, I. (1996) *How to organise a conference*, Aldershot, Gower, pp. 40–50.

Poorani, A.A. (1996) Trade Show Management. *Cornell Hotel and Restaurant Administration Quarterly*, August, pp. 77–84.

Seekings, D. (1996) *How to organise effective conferences and meetings*, London, Kogan Page, pp. 30–81.

Smyth, H. (1994) *Marketing the City: The role of flagship development in urban regeneration*, London, E&FN Spon, pp. 127–161.

11

Conference planning

The aims of this chapter are:

1 To explore issues relating to conference planning.
2 To consider the role of the conference staff in the planning and operational processes of a conference.

11.1 Introduction

The single most important aspect of the operation of a conference centre is, arguably, the conference planning process. This is the basis of good conference management and a measure of the efficiency with which a conference should be handled. It is vital to providing both a good experience for delegates and a professional approach to organizers.

The main players involved in the process are the client, in the form of the conference organizer or booking agent, and the sales and operational teams of the conference venue. Titles are often confusing, but for consistency of approach here, we will assume that the person in the sales team dealing with the enquiry stage will be the sales manager; the person dealing with the confirmed booking and preparation for the event will be the event manager; and the person dealing with the conference on the day will be the floor manager. Organizations vary, but Figure 11.1 provides a comparison of this process between a purpose-built conference centre and a hotel venue.

11.2   Enquiries and provisional bookings

Selling the facilities of a conference centre itself is the first stage in a process leading to running the actual event. The planning process and the efficiency with which the planning is done is extremely important in ensuring that the conference organizer and delegates get what they want. A conference should not be, at first sight, difficult to arrange or to manage. The provision of a meeting room and refreshments does not necessarily involve great complexity. On the other hand, regular conference delegates will be well aware of the wide range of things that can (and do) go wrong during a conference (Taylor, 1988). Typically, problems are due to a lack of planning, forethought or poor organization and management on the day.

In order to ensure that the planning process is efficient, it should ideally comprise a series of steps. Starting with the enquiry from the client, which may be a conference organizer or an agency, the sales manager must ensure that all the information needed for a successful event has been accumulated and that the conference organizer's wishes have been fully explored (Kotler et al., 1996) (Hartley and Witt, 1994). It is important to that while a conference organizer may be experienced in dealing with conference centres, as too will agencies, these do not make up the total of all clients using a centre. Some clients may be regulars or have experienced organizers on their staff or employ an agency or production company to do the work; some clients will be organizations with no conference experience or who have delegated the job of the conference organization to a new or inexperienced member of staff. Thus, in dealing with a client it is important for the venue to know whether the client's organizer is experienced or not, as this determines how much help and advice he or she may need in arranging the conference.

If the enquiry is new business, or if the organizer is new to booking conferences, there is a set of steps that the venue can take to ensure the planning process is effective. At the point of enquiry, which may be by phone, fax, e-mail or in person, a number of details must be taken about the conference, though at an early stage not all details will be known. The most crucial details are the date of the event; the number of delegates; the number of days; whether the event will be residential or non-residential; the name of the organizer (which may be a company contact or an agent booker); the address and phone number of the client contact (Strick and Montgomery, 1995; Seekings, 1996). This is just the beginning, but these details form the bare bones of the information needed about the conference –

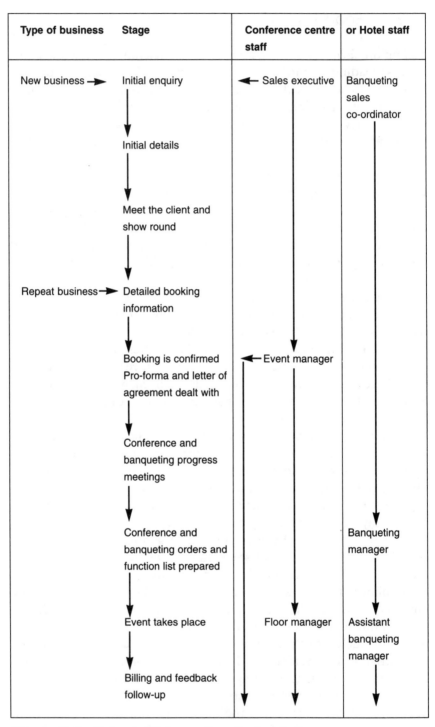

Figure 11.1 Example of the conference planning process

when it is, to identify whether the venue has availability; how many delegates, to identify whether the venue has appropriate or large enough rooms; the number of days, to determine whether the rooms are available throughout the proposed event; whether the event is residential or non-residential, and if residential, to ensure bedroom accommodation is also available at the same time, either in-house (if a hotel or residential centre) or elsewhere, if the conference centre is non-residential or the in-house bedroom accommodation is fully booked (and to ensure the proposed bedroom accommodation arrangements are acceptable to the client); the name and address of the organizer or booker, for contact purposes.

In the early stages of the planning process, some organizers will have a fairly comprehensive idea of their needs, some organizers will not. Therefore, in addition to the basic details, a range of other information must be sought, either at the enquiry stage or at a show-round for the organizer. More details may be accumulated as the conference planning process develops, either through the client knowing more about their needs, or in response to the venue asking questions and seeking information about an organizer's plans. If we were to take as an example a large purpose-built conference centre, such as the Brewery Centre in London, the planning process is effectively undertaken by three people: a sales manager, who receives the initial enquiry, deals with a show-round and enters all the preliminary information while an enquiry is provisional; an event manager who is responsible for the conference once the provisional enquiry becomes a confirmed booking, and who will finalize details and deal with the immediate run-up to the conference; and a floor manager who will actually run the event on the day.

The sales manager, having taken the initial enquiry, and checked availability of rooms and other major needs on the proposed dates, will then begin to explore the further details needed for the event. Normally a show-round will take place, with the conference organizer visiting the venue. Sometimes the conference organizer may bring other members of the client organization with him/her, for example the senior manager whose budget will pay for the conference. In the early stages clients may well visit more than one venue before taking a decision. Therefore the show-round is not only an opportunity for the venue to seek more information but also to convince the organizer that this venue is the right one. Show-rounds must be carefully managed to achieve the best outcome. It is not simply a matter of asking the client for more details and saying 'here is the room you are likely to use'. Clients should be able to see all the facilities: reception/delegate check-in area, the conference room itself, the areas to be used for dining and hospitality, the business centre if one exists and, in the case of a residential conference, a delegate bedroom. Sales staff in conference venues should expect clients being shown round to be methodical, even awkward. The more care taken at this stage to ensure everything is suitable, the greater the likelihood of a more successful event later. Experienced conference organizers will be better at this and will, when being shown round, know what questions to ask related to their enquiry and the needs of their conference. Less experienced organizers may not only need more help and more careful prompting, but may have to be encouraged to ask questions they might feel 'are not important enough' but in practice could make or break the event. Some conference organizers will bring checklists and run through these as they are taken round, many will not and will have to be encouraged to give details needed. First impressions count and organizers must not be kept waiting for their show-round. Many, being experienced, may ask seemingly obscure questions, 'Where are the lavatories?', 'Can I sit in one of your chairs?' and so on. Some judge a venue not on the condition of the conference rooms but on the preparedness of the sales manager – Has the sales manager asked about special requests? Has the sales manager read the initial details properly? These are important because they are an indication of the professionalism of the conference venue. Not all venues are professional enough or prepared enough. In attempting to sell a venue to a client, the sales manager must not only be able to see his/her venue through the client's eyes, but must also be in a position to do something about it. It is therefore important, when expecting a show-round visit, not only to be on time, but also to have checked the obvious things that the client will see. Go outside and check the parking area and the entrance – Is it clean? Do the lights work? Does reception know a visitor is expected? Check the rooms to be seen – Is everything working? Are the toilets clean? In addition to the physical there is also the issue of expectations. The client expects the sales manager to be professional in outlook and appearance; he/she expects the sales manager to know his/her details so issues can be explored and more information exchanged. Some venues will seek to utilize the show-round more effectively than others; show-rounds may, for example, include demonstrations of AVA (audio visual aids) equipment if that has been a special request, or may include tastings of food or wine if these have been identified as important to the client.

The further details to be worked out for an event are quite wide ranging and crucial to the success of the event overall. Normally, details would include further information about the event itself: Is it a training event? A VIP meeting? A presentation? This gives the venue and the sales manager a clearer idea of requirements and the standards to be achieved. There would be further contact details, above and beyond the address, usually to include a fax number and perhaps the name of the client's contact on the day if this person differs from the conference organizer.

Meeting-related information would include times of arrival and departure, and numbers, as the meeting might be more than one event in one room; for example, a pre-meeting of senior managers, followed by the main conference plenary and then by several smaller breakout sessions. Each has to be timed and rooms allocated. Breakouts are often a problem because of the possible shortage of smaller seminar rooms and also due to conference organizers' tendency to not plan the meeting format sufficiently in advance or to identify how may breakout rooms may be needed at any one time. From this information the sales manager, the event manager and the floor manager can consider set-up and breakdown times for the various rooms needed, arrangements for delegate reception and any special requirements.

Catering information would also include times of refreshments, whether these are short refreshment breaks or main meals, the number of delegates taking refreshment at each point and the details of the refreshment itself. This information may be developed out of standard menu suggestions for each meal, or by liaison with the venue's chef. Simple refreshment breaks may consist only of tea/coffee and biscuits; others may range up to gala dinners following a conference. As noted from the show-round, conference organizers may wish to have a taste test of the suggested dishes on behalf of the client. Menu planning must not only take into account the budget available, but also special requests and unusual dietary requirements. These details will be used by the venue chef to prepare the food order, by the dispense bar staff to prepare wine, drinks or other beverage order, by the operations staff to order linen, napkins etc. and to have menus and place cards printed, as well as a whole range of other considerations which flow from the client's decision on the menu, ranging from the staffing requirements of the service to the need for special lighting or other items.

Presentation details should include outline information on the speakers or presenters the client wishes to have, how many and when they would be speaking. With a series of speakers there may be an outline time schedule of approximately who will speak when. Experience shows that time schedules for speakers are often unrealistic for a range of reasons, most simply speakers' lack of ability to stick to their scheduled time allocation. More importantly from the venue's point of view is the type of audio visual equipment requested by the conference organizer for the speakers. This may range from the simple overhead projector and screen to the most complicated state-of-the-art multimedia equipment. Sales managers and event managers should take care to check that they are, however, talking about the same type of equipment that conference organizers have in mind. The less experienced organizer may ask for a projector, thinking that his/her managing director wants a 35 mm slide projector, and the event manager may reserve an overhead projector (OHP), thinking that this is what is meant by 'projector', when in practice the managing director might really have wanted a back projection unit to show a video. Technology is constantly changing and as a consequence it is now common for event managers to ask the client to come in and rehearse with the proposed equipment, if this is in any way technical. Much embarrassment and time of organizers and delegates can be saved, and the venue seen to be more professional, if the hi-tech computer equipment brought in (at much trouble and cost) actually works, rather than being found to be incompatible with the venue's system or its power supply, or impossible to get through the doors.

The meeting, catering and presentational information are crucial to the operation of the conference on the day, but three other categories of information are needed in the preliminary stages. In all cases, accounting or billing information is needed, or more simply, to whom the bill is to be sent. Terms and conditions of booking will dictate when payments, such as a deposit, have to be paid, what cancellation charges exist and what the payment terms are. Normally, a letter of agreement would be signed at the confirmation stage, which will specify basic information, terms and conditions and the charges.

In the case of residential conferences, whether the residential element (delegate bedrooms) are provided in-house or externally, it will be necessary to know how many bedrooms are required, when, and of what type – single, double or twin. Most conference business requires single occupancy, though certain types of conference allow for spouses or even for delegates sharing twin rooms (this latter is sometimes used to keep costs down, but may not be attractive to delegates). Costs must be made clear to the conference organizer, and if the accommodation is not on-site then arrangements for getting delegates from their hotel(s) to the conference centre should be discussed, even if simply to identify that delegates would make their own transport arrangements (or that transport is needed).

Finally, in the case of incentive conferences, or ones with special events, leisure or spousal programmes included, details will be needed about activities for leisure and recreation (such as the use of an in-house leisure centre, golf course or fitness suite, by delegates) or for arrangements to be made to use nearby facilities or prepare tour or transport itineraries for visits to local attractions, shopping areas or entertainment.

11.3   Confirmed bookings and preparation

All these details will be recorded, probably on computer with a manual backup record, the manual system being a pro-forma booking sheet which is then filed. The pro-formas are probably duplicated and may consist of three copies: one for a master file (by alphabetical order of organization name), one for a trace file (by date order) and one for reference purposes by the manager who will supervise the event.

At some point after the show-round and after the fuller details have been taken, confirmation of the provisional arrangements and a booking deposit should be received. The process is likely to generate other necessary paperwork. At the point of enquiry the conference centre may respond to the enquiry with a formal letter and a brochure pack, which may contain both hard copy and, from some venues, a CD-ROM. This may be followed by a further letter confirming the show-round and clarifying simple details. Once the show-round has taken place, a further letter quoting prices for the arrangements discussed would be sent. At some point after this, the client, if satisfied with arrangements, will confirm in writing and with a deposit. A number of conference centres also provide letters of agreement such as an event reservation form. This will specify outline costs for the event and terms and conditions for the booking; for cancellation arrangements; for charges; for timing of payment; requirements relating to the use of the premises; property; damage; insurance and liabilities.

Naturally, not all enquiries or show-rounds will generate bookings and many centres may follow up initial enquiries and show-rounds with a phone call to see if a booking is likely or not, and in the case of the latter, to obtain feedback on what reasons might be evident for not getting the booking. Confirmation having been made and the event reservation form signed by both parties, further work will take place at the conference centre, under the control of the event manager (or in the case of hotels, under the control of a banqueting sales co-ordinator). Routine preparation for events will probably be a weekly meeting of team leaders, including the operations and sales staff, the head chef and venue manager. This will be to review all events for the following week and will be preceded by the preparation of a set of weekly function sheets (see Figure 11.2). Generally, function sheets run from Monday to Sunday and will be prepared on the Tuesday of the preceding week, with the routine weekly planning meeting on the Wednesday. This meeting will also deal with the more advanced requirements of food and liquor requests two weeks prior to the event, to allow sufficient ordering time, and will also address non-routine issues or special requests which may have a far longer lead time. The other routine element of preparation for events will probably be a daily early morning meeting, of the short and sharp type, to ensure that all that day's events are in hand and any last-minute requests from organizers are conveyed to floor managers (or in the case of hotels, the assistant banqueting manager running that particular conference).

The weekly function sheets, sometimes called 'banqueting event orders', are extremely important in the planning process in the run-up to the event. These sheets will comprise all the information needed by all departments for the week's events, and care must be taken to ensure accuracy. The sheets will be made up from the booking details and may be taken from the booking information and separately written up, or may use a copy of the function booking pro-forma (the latter is more common as it prevents errors occurring in writing up the details from the file to the function sheets). Thus the complete set of function sheets, for any given week, will consist of information on several events. Once a full set of sheets has been prepared for the following week, enough copies must be made for every department, not just for the event managers. For example, the kitchen has to know final meal selection; the housekeeper has to know numbers and layouts to provide linen; the technical staff have to know what presentation equipment is needed and in which room. The more complicated an event, the more people are involved and the greater the need for accuracy, good communication and attention to detail. A wedding, or a large themed gala banquet, may need four times the effort in

SHORELINE CONFERENCE CENTRE

**Residential conference facilities for 200/Computer LCD and
video projection/Video conferencing/Sound systems/Business support**

Shoreline Conference Centre: Marine Parade East, Fiction on Sea, Essex CO00 0OO
Phone: 00000 718309 Fax: 00000 718388 E-mail: shore@mail.rmplc.co.uk

Type of event: *Annual Conference*   **Date(s): 11th and 12th May 1998**

Your contact: *James Davies on 01000 255137*

Our contact: *Rob Johnson on 01000 718309*

Room: *Connaught Room (conference)*

Langtry Room (Gala dinner)

Start time: 09.00 on the 11th   **Finish time: 17.00 approx on the 11th**
Same both days

Number of delegates: Max 120   **Number for lunch: 120**
Number for dinner 200

Lunch menu: *Finger buffet no 1 both days* **Wine: to be confirmed**
Dinner menu: *Dinner menu no 2 on the 11th*
Gala dinner menu (to follow)

Other refreshments: *Tea/Coffee on arrival at 09.00*
Tea/Coffee and biscuits at 10.45
Tea/Coffee and pastries at 15.00

Room Lay-up: *Conference: Theatre style*   *Staff for information:*
Dinner: Cabaret style   *Sharon Wright*
Hans Reiser
Mineral water/Orange squash Kevin Gentry
Conference pads   *Mavis Diss*
Table mints   *Tracey Bambrick*
Luigi Ginolla

Special Equipment: *Video*
OHP and Screen
Flipchart

Car parking: *None reserved*

This account: *Payment in advance, as agreed*

Any other remarks/special requests:

_____
_____
_____

Figure 11.2 Example of the information to be found on a function sheet

planning and organizing than a straightforward day conference for 20 delegates.

On the day of the conference, this whole process then depends on the efficiency and ability of the staff and the floor manager (or in hotels, the assistant banqueting manager) to ensure that the meeting room is prepared and laid up properly; that refreshments are delivered and available on time; that the conference organizer doesn't have to chase around for minor requirements; essentially that everything goes according to the details specified. This said, experienced conference managers will recognize just how often things may not go according to plan. Last-minute alterations and requests, forgotten in the planning stage (often by the clients), can ruin a conference and the reputation of the conference centre. Floor managers must be able to use their initiative and act on their feet. Not all clients are well organized and not all organizers know what they are doing. Often an organization's managing director turns up to 'his' or 'her' conference and a whole series of things get changed or crop up because the expectations of the person paying the bill differ from those of the person who did the organizing. This is the nature of the activity; every day is different and the conference business is not a production line.

As the event draws to a close, it is important not only that the floor manager remains available, but also that the event manager responsible for the final stages of planning for that conference is available to follow up on the day's activities. A short chat with the organizer and perhaps a few delegates should identify how well, or not, the event has gone. Further, more formalized follow-up could take place, in the form of a questionnaire or call to the organizer when time is less pressing.

Summary

The cornerstone of the activity of conference venues is the careful planning of each event. The unique nature of conferences, each one different, means that this process, though routine and systematic in approach, must be capable of dealing with a very wide range of demands, contingencies, special requests and unusual occurrences. The more careful the planning, the greater the chance of both a smoothly run conference and its success in the eyes of the clients.

References

Astroff, M.T. and Abbey, J.R. (1991) *Convention Sales and Services*, New Jersey, USA, Waterbury Press, pp. 253–265.

Hartley, J.S. and Witt, S.F. (1994) Increasing the conversion rate of conference and function enquiries into sales. *International Journal of Hospitality Management*, **13**(3), pp. 275–285.

Kotler, P., Bowen, J. and Makins, S. (1996) *Marketing for Hospitality and Tourism*, London, Prentice-Hall, pp. 217–236.

Maitland, I. (1996) *How to organise a conference*, Aldershot, Gower, pp. 40–50.

Seekings, D. (1996) *How to organise effective conferences and meetings*, London, Kogan Page, 6th edn, pp. 356–367.

Strick, S.K. and Montgomery, R.J. (1995) *Meetings, Conventions and Expositions*, New York, Van Nostrand Reinhold, pp. 160–189.

Taylor, D. (1988) *Hotel and Catering Sales*, Oxford, Heinemann, pp. 196–214.

12

Trends _____

The aims of this chapter are:

1 To examine the factors which drive change in the conference business.
2 To consider the effects these factors may have on the development of the conference business in the future.

12.1   Introduction

The conference business has undergone, and continues to undergo, rapid change. The expansion of conferencing as an activity appears to have gone hand-in-hand with the structural changes in the UK and Irish economies, from manufacturing to service based; in consequence, the UK has one of the most well-developed conference industries in Europe and Ireland's conference industry is developing rapidly. There is no general perception that conferencing is an industry, however, as it is largely subsumed into the hospitality and tourism industries. This perception is changing nevertheless, partly due to a general expansion in demand and partly due to the increasing maturity of professional and other industry bodies. Many factors will impinge on the future development of the industry, from changes in social attitudes to technological development and changes in the economic and business environment.

12.2   Social change

Conference buyers and delegates are just as much part of a changing society as any other client group; consequently, it is necessary to look at some of the issues of wider social change, as these impinge on the attitudes, the outlook and the decision-making process of organizers and delegates. Awareness of social change and its effect should inform the judgement of venue managers about the services, styles, standards and provision needed within conference centres in the future (Hirst, 1996).

The cosmopolitan delegate

Conference delegates (and organizers) are becoming more cosmopolitan in their outlook. In the past when people only took holidays in the UK or in Ireland (e.g. at seaside resorts) they tended to be less comfortable attending conferences outside the country. Today, and in the future, organizers and delegates are well travelled, and younger people, in particular, do not view a European conference destination, for example, as being 'foreign'. The increasing influence of travel is crucial to this; previously, a client might only have considered a location within the UK or Ireland; in future, mainland Europe and particularly destinations such as Paris and Brussels will offer increasing competition.

Changing delegate profiles

The nature of the workforce, particularly in the service sector of the economy, which generates significant demand for the conference business, has increasingly moved from a male-dominated profile to a balance of delegates, both male and female. This impacts on the nature of services that conference venues must provide, including more secure parking, the provision of crèche facilities, the menu composition of the catering, through to the ambience of conference rooms themselves. These things are often not sufficiently explored by venues, which are relatively poor at piloting activities such as refurbishment and new menus to take account of their changing delegate profile.

Delegates' time is short

The UK has the highest average number of working hours per week of any country in the EU (Drake, 1994). Delegates themselves are short of time (as conferences are often compressed into short periods), above and beyond the simple limitations of how much time a conference organizer might allow for conference sessions. This means that delegates are often virtually 'captive' within conference centres and the provision of services must take this into account. Business support, such as copying and faxing, must be responsive and on the spot – 'some time this afternoon' is not good enough. Ancillary activities such as the coffee shop or the in-house store must be capable of speedy service and of providing the right goods – most conference centres are still incapable of supplying delegates with a pint of milk to take home or anything at all after 5.00 p.m. If delegates are genuinely short of time, basic amenities of this kind and opening times when delegates break or finish are a vital and a necessary part of the quality of service delegates will expect.

The knock-on effects of delegates being harried for time has implications for core aspects of the service too – rooms must be ready on time, must be serviced promptly when sessions break and elements such as registration must be, above all, fast. Queuing for 30 minutes to register is unacceptable, as it implies that the delegate must arrive earlier, impinging on his/her private time. Similarly, it may, at the opposite end of the day, be more time effective for a delegate to take an evening meal on the premises rather than go hunting for a restaurant or a bar in the town – provided the ambience and standards of the in-house facilities are up to the job. The art is to add value to the basic activity of the conference – even if this adding of value is a matter of providing services which help reduce delegates' time in travelling or time acquiring additional goods or services.

The informed organizer

The conference business has expanded rapidly during the past 20 years. Whereas in the past, a person might only attend a conference very occasionally, the awareness and education of conference organizers and delegates has increased significantly – organizers are more experienced and professional, delegates have been to many conferences and have higher expectations (Swarbrooke, 1995). The effect has been to create a more aware, better informed client base. This, coupled with a high level of competition, can result in a very low level of loyalty towards a venue and high levels of transferability, i.e. conferences ceasing to be regular at a given venue because the standards do not match the competition; organizers 'head for the exit' – go somewhere else. This creates a need, not only for more consistent and higher standards, but for better relations between venue managers, organizers and delegates. Crucial to this relationship is the ability of the venue and floor management to be seen and talked to during conferences, at session breaks and at the start and end of events. Without this, interaction and feedback are poor and a simple problem which could have been remedied by the venue manager on the spot (had he/she been there) may result in the loss of the whole conference (Lovelock, 1994).

12.3   Design and technology issues

Contemporary design issues in conference centre development are varied, but fall into the following categories.

Access

Current wisdom is that buildings should be designed to cope with the least able potential users, not the most. In essence, if a doorway is designed to cope with (for example) wheelchair access, it will be just as useful for fully mobile visitors and delegates, but the same is clearly not true vice versa. In this way, by addressing access issues from the point of view of least able users, all can be accommodated.

Health and safety

Increasing attention has been given to health and safety issues and their related design requirements, the rule of 'reasonable achievability' being applied, which has been learned from risk analysis of disasters. The key question is the extent to which health and safety design factors have a cost–benefit in reducing potential problems and at what point the laws of diminishing return begin to apply, or even at what point over-emphasis on safety both negates original use and becomes counter productive. (An example is the over-signing of roads, or exit routes around a building, there being anecdotal evi-

dence that the excessive use of road signs, in particular, is a distrac-
tion to drivers, this negating the very safety issues they are intended
to guard.) Internal signing and design may fall into the same category – do signs for escape routes genuinely stand out from the
plethora of other signs giving information, adverts, general furniture
and the crush of people? This should lead to a move for the simpli-
fication of signing, perhaps by the increased use of icons, capable of
delivering the same message to delegates with varying language back-
grounds, but still maintaining the emphasis on safety without confu-
sion.

Fire

The nature of conference centre design is of large open areas, in
terms of large-scale and often raked rooms, together with extensive
circulation areas (especially atria) which require specialist fire prevention and protection systems. The historic approach to building
fire prevention has been compartmentalization and containment, but
modern conference hall design may not directly achieve this. The
issue of design in response to the threat of fire does, therefore,
require the full attention of architects and operators. Recent legislation for this field is covered in the European Framework and
Workplace Directives, enacted in the UK in the Fire Precautions
(Workplace) Regulations 1997 and similar legislation in Ireland.

Security

The single most forgotten factor of security for conference and convention centres is that, almost without exception, these are public
buildings. As such the public cannot and, as a generality, should not
be excluded from the chief circulation areas such as the foyers. The
difficulty is to achieve the necessary openness. After all, some visitors
will be potential buyers who wish to gain an impression of a centre
while retaining their anonymity.

The need for security sometimes leads to over-intrusiveness. It is
essential that delegates do not feel their privacy is intruded upon.
While equipment such as video cameras may be present in public
areas, it must not, for reasons of confidentiality, be present in
meeting rooms themselves. It must also be understood that surveillance is not of itself the genuine provider of security, merely an

element of a whole, which may include security personnel, specialist equipment (e.g. metal detectors) even, design issues such as good lighting, ease of exit (though clearly not necessarily of entry) and design tranquillity of the building itself.

Design pilot schemes

As a generality, wherever possible, new aspects of design such as the colour scheme of a breakout room, new air conditioning or other technical equipment etc., should be piloted first. If a full refurbishment or re-equipping programme is envisaged, venues should try it for a suitable period in one room first or see it in operation elsewhere. It is far too common that delegates arrive for their conference to find that the chairs are uncomfortable, tables wobble, lights flicker, air conditioning is noisy, room decor is claustrophobic and by a fluke of the building conduits you can hear the chef blow his nose half a kilometre away, in the middle of the President's address. Piloting should enable at least some of these problems to be prevented: involve the delegates.

Impact of video and desktop conferencing

Some debate has taken place about the impact of technology such as video- and desktop-conferencing on the conference business as a whole – will, on the one hand, improving technology render conferences unnecessary? If you can desktop-conference to business colleagues anywhere in the world, will you still need to travel to see them? Or would such techniques actually stimulate demand for greater conferencing? In all probability, these arguments take too narrow a view of the nature of the conferencing business. We noted, when introducing the history of the conference business, that while the exchange of ideas is a core function of conferences and meetings, it is not the sole function. There is a significant social element. Conferences are really only a formalized version of social interaction. In so far as delegates to conferences are present not only for the exchange of information, but also for social activities like networking, then the technology of video- and desktop-conferencing cannot hope to take over the wider role, merely act as subsidiary or complementary to it. Without a doubt, conference venues should also provide video and desktop conferencing facilities, as these can be seen as a vital business support function, but technological facilities cannot achieve the social role of a conference itself, from informal chats with competitors in the corridors between session breaks, to a drink in the bar afterwards to reflect on the issues. It is necessary to be realistic about what technology can achieve; it is often the case that proponents of technology have an over-optimistic view of the extent of its impact and an insufficient consideration of the social implications.

12.4   Change in the business environment

Just as much as social change is rapid in the modern world, so too is change in the business environment. In some respects the two are closely interlinked. Changes in the business environment may be driven by a range of factors, including economic, legal or market issues which are sometimes difficult to disentangle, and range from the global to the local.

The competitive environment

Historically, the competitive environment for the conference business has been confined to the various sectors within the domestic economy, with the international market being largely separate, and only a few major venues in the UK and Ireland competing for market share internationally. This pattern is beginning to change globally, and regionally within Europe. Globally, a number of locations have had a strongly developed provision, notably the USA, with Hawaii being a major destination. Increasingly the countries of the Pacific Rim are developing conference provision, although as many of these economies are predominantly manufacturing based, it is not yet a significant competitive issue. Venues in Britain and Ireland are, however, competing much more actively for business in Europe, as are conference venues in Europe looking at UK and Irish markets. This is due to the gradual elimination of barriers to travel around Europe and developments such as the Eurostar network and fast ferries between mainland Europe, the UK and Ireland. Increasingly, the 'international' market (in so far as it refers to Europe) will become the domestic one, and it is important to our perception of the market that this is clearly understood.

Investment

In as much as the competitive environment is changing, so too is the investment environment. After a hiatus, in the early 1990s, companies are once again investing heavily in hospitality, tourism and conference businesses. Bearing in mind that the hotel sector is a major provider of conference facilities, it follows that the development of mid-market and de luxe hotels will, more or less naturally, expand the provision of conference facilities. As much is true of the academic sector, which, under increasing financial pressure from government, is seeking additional sources of revenue. The major universities, in particular, have invested significant amounts in conference centres in order to develop conferences as a revenue stream, although some recent evidence indicates this part of the market may be less fast growing than others (Richards, 1996). In terms of purpose-built centres, the picture is rather different. During the economic boom of the late 1980s a number of flagship purpose-built conference centres were conceived with a high proportion of private sector funding (i.e. debt), in contrast to the more common (previous) method of civic funding from councils or from share issues (i.e. equity). This was, though, rather short lived and since 1990 the investment pattern for such flagship developments has tended to involve a balance of funds from various sources, both debt and equity. In addition, other forms of development funds have been sought from civic, governmental or European fields (Hansen, 1995) including the European Regional Development Fund. Finally, the arrival of the National Lottery in the UK in the mid-1990s, and the provision of Lottery money for a range of projects in many fields including sport, heritage and the arts, resulted in a number of applications for multi-purpose developments, in which conferencing was one component. It is arguable, in the last category, and also as a generality, that the provision of large purpose-built conference centres is now at a mature level, given that the demand for mega-conferences is limited, but that smaller cities and towns may well seek to gain a share of the extensive smaller conference market by multi-purpose provision, or perhaps by the creation of mini-centres providing facilities for conferences of up to 200 people, leisure facilities and basic support such as a coffee shop, limited retail facilities, small business centres and adequate secure parking.

Investment may also be considered to be less parochial than in the past, in the sense that, with the breakdown of national barriers and the increasing number of international organizations, investment funding in facilities in the future is just as much likely to originate from another country as it is from within the UK or Ireland.

My space or yours?

One of the characteristics of the way in which organizations have changed during the past ten years in the private sector, and probably will change in the next ten years in the public sector, has been the delayering of management and downsizing of the organization itself, the net result being a reduction in space requirements. Hand-in-hand with this has gone the ability to put an organization's space requirements under the microscope, as the costs of running and maintaining property are substantial. While some organizations have created in-house conference centres in order to reduce the cost of organizing conferences elsewhere, be it in hotels, academic centres or wherever, the effort of doing so can only be justified if these centres are cost-effective for the amount of use they get. On the flip side are those organizations that have downsized and also eliminated much of their property, thus requiring conference space elsewhere, and increasing demand. Received wisdom at present (Hirst, 1996) is that demand increases will continue, many organizations having a reduced ability to provide in-house conferences and meetings. Linked to this, from the point of view of conference centre managers, is their own ability to use the space within the venue effectively. The effectiveness of space use is not a matter of finding the 'right size' of conference and 'packing them in' but more a question of flexibility of use related to satisfying demand, sometimes called 'chameleon space' or put more simply, the ability to do a 100-delegate conference one day and 4 x 25 delegate conferences the next, in the same space. It is the optimization of space that matters, relating back to earlier points made about the asset management of venues.

Impact of increased flexibility of working

As organizations have downsized, some have sought to create greater flexibility of working for their workforce with techniques such as hot desking and homeworking to reduce demand on the property (or expensive space) which an organization needs (Gorman and Bown, 1990), though often at a cost of providing higher levels of technology such as workstations, laptop computers, modems, e-mail and

Web links. Given the points made earlier about the networking role of conferences, the social interaction aspects of conferences are also significant when considering the needs of organizations which are fragmented. The provision of conferences and meetings is a means of maintaining the social fabric of an organization. In consequence, in those organizations there may well be an increased demand for conferences. This also has implications for conference organizers in terms of how to structure conferences so that interaction opportunities are maximized, which may lead to shorter plenary sessions and a higher level of interactive and informal slots in the programme.

Increasing service sector and professional employment

Both the UK and Irish economies have gradually become more service dominated. As this has occurred, the level of skills and knowledge in large sections of the workforce has had to increase. In a competitive environment it is of considerable importance for organizations and individuals to continue their education, which, put in simple terms, is likely to increase the need for seminars, training meetings and a whole range of other conference and convention activity. Although some of this demand is soaked up by academic institutions in the provision of new courses, the re-skilling of the workforce has seen an increase in demand from seminar and training organizations for conference facilities.

Summary

The pace of change in the conference business has increased in recent years, particularly with the impact of new technology. Nevertheless, we must not forget that conferencing is primarily a social activity, and one which is crucial to the interchange of ideas. As such, the business has a bright future, but needs good management and organizational skills as much as any other industry. It is hoped that this book goes some way to laying the foundation for those skills.

References

Drake, G. (1994) *Issues in the New Europe*, London, Hodder and Stoughton, pp. 64–72, 252–265.

Gorman, F. and Bown, C. (1990) *The Responsive Office*, Streatley, Polymath, pp. 31–46.

Grundy, C. (1996) *What are the Issues?*, European Hospitality Management Conference, 25 March, Amsterdam, HCIMA (Conference paper).

Hansen, K. (1995) Serving a Purpose. *Conference and Incentive Travel Magazine*, July/August. pp.15–22.

Hirst, M. (1996) *Hospitality into the 21st Century, a vision for the future*, Henley, The Henley Centre, pp. 6–42.

Keynote (1994) *Keynote Report: A Market Sector Overview: Exhibitions and Conferences*, London, Keynote Publications, pp. 29–37.

Lovelock, C.H. (1994) *Product Plus*, New York, McGraw-Hill, pp. 206–222.

Michels, D. (1996) *The Annual Savoy Lecture: The Future of the Hospitality Industry*, Annual Savoy Lecture, London, Savoy Trust.

Richards, B. (1996) The Conference Market in the UK. In *Insights*, London, English Tourist Board, pp. B67–B83.

Slattery, P., Feehely, G. and Savage, M. (1995) *The Leisure and Hotels Sector: Quo Vadis?*, London, Kleinwort Benson Research.

Swarbrooke, J. (1995) *The Development and Management of Visitor Attractions*, Oxford, Butterworth-Heinemann, pp. 351–371.

Glossary

Assembly
Is normally a large group of people gathered for deliberation, legislation, worship, lobbying or some political activity.

Breakout session
Where small groups formed from the delegates of a larger event work together, usually in separate areas or rooms.

Buyer
A person (or sometimes a group of people) who hold responsibility for the purchasing of conference services within an organization.

Cash bar
A bar set up during a function where the guests or delegates, rather than the host, pay for drinks individually.

Colloquium
This is an academic meeting at which one or more academic specialists or researchers deliver lectures on a topic and then answer questions about it.

Conclave
A private meeting or assembly often, though not exclusively, of a religious nature.

Concurrent sessions
When sessions of a meeting are held at the same time in different rooms, usually allowing delegates to choose which to attend.

Conference
In the UK and Ireland the word 'conference' is used to describe almost any type of meeting whose purpose is the interchange of ideas.

The Meeting Industry Association (1996) define a conference as 'An event involving 10 or more people for a minimum of four hours during one day or more, frequently held outside the company's own premises'. However, this definition has some flaws – first it does not address the question of 'doing what?' or 'what sort of event?' and secondly it supposes, erroneously, that all conferences are company events.

Coopers and Lybrand Deloitte (1990) take the dictionary definition as 'A meeting of two or more people for the discussion of matters of common concern/a formal exchange of ideas.'

Conference organizers often use the word 'conference' to describe events with over 50 people, 'meeting' to describe those with fewer. In hotels the word 'conference' is used to describe almost any meeting of whatever size. In the USA, the word 'convention' is preferred, and in continental Europe 'congress' is the general usage.

Convention

In the UK and Ireland the word 'convention' implies a gathering of greater importance than a normal conference, in terms of size and formality, perhaps an event with over 300 people in attendance.

Corporate hospitality

Corporate hospitality (or 'corporate entertaining') involves inviting groups of people, usually clients or staff of an organization, to public events such as rugby at Twickenham, the Farnborough Airshow or racing at Leopardstown, or to private activities (such as paintballing, car racing or hot air ballooning) at the organization's expense.

Cut-off date

The designated date when a conference organizer must release reserved, but unconfirmed meeting room or banqueting space.

Day delegate rate

Is the price quoted by conference venues for providing one delegate with meeting facilities, refreshments, such as morning coffee, lunch and afternoon tea, normally for one 8.30 a.m. to 5.30 p.m. session, including VAT. (The 24 hour rate would include all the above, plus overnight accommodation, breakfast and dinner.)

Delegates

The main term used to describe people who attend conferences, seminars and similar events. See also 'participants' and 'guests'.

Delegate day
This is a measure of the number of people attending a conference each day. Thus, 10 people attending a conference for one day is 10 delegate days.

'External' events
An event arranged by an organization, particularly in the corporate market, to disseminate information to external audiences (e.g. to wholesalers, distributors, dealers, consumers, the press).

Guaranteed number
The minimum number of guests or delegates at an event for which the host has paid or will pay, irrespective of the actual number to attend.

Guest
A person staying at a hotel or residential conference venue, who may or may not also be a conference delegate.

Head count
The actual number of people attending a conference, function or event.

Incentive
An event designed to be a perk or reward for staff in an organization. Although some incentives have a serious element, the principal purpose is to motivate, encourage or reward. Incentives are often for salespeople and, frequently, their partners.

'Internal' events
These are events where attendance is confined to personnel inside the organization, such as the sales force, workforce, departments and groups and people attending internal – as opposed to external – training courses, thus 'in-house' or 'in-company').

Letter of agreement
A document which confirms all the requirements, services and costs as agreed between the conference organizer and the venue. In effect a contract for the event.

Meeting
A meeting is usually a smaller event of perhaps, at most, 50 people,

usually fewer. However, the word 'meetings' is also used in a wider sense to describe conferences, meetings and seminars in a collective manner.

Moderator
A conference moderator is a person who chairs or guides a large-scale conference. This may be a person from within the organization, a professional moderator or sometimes a celebrity, whose role is to guide and stimulate the conference debate or panel session.

Panel session
Part of a conference debate where questions may be asked of a 'top table' or panel of experts from the floor (i.e. delegate's question time).

Participant
Similar to the term 'delegate', but used particularly for people attending training programmes.

Plenary
Part of a conference at which all delegates are present.

Poster session
A session allowed in major conferences where authors or researchers of papers which are not presented in conference stand by noticeboards displaying abstracts of their papers ready to meet delegates and answer questions, often found at academic or research conferences.

Pre-con meeting
A meeting between the conference organizer and the sales co-ordinator or floor manager to confirm details just prior to the event.

Presentation
This word is sometimes used as an alternative to 'conference' or 'meeting', but more usually to describe the formal process of telling the audience something.

Product launch
A 'show' to introduce an audience such as the media to a new product or service. It may also be aimed at an organization's internal management and staff, sales force or external dealers and customers.

Programme
The schedule of events within a conference.

Public event
An event attended by members of the general public.

Road show
Is where the same event is staged in several different geographical locations.

Seminar
Describes small gatherings similar to the breakout sessions, where a group, not the whole plenary, will discuss an issue.

Session
The word used to describe an unbroken period within a conference.

Summit
A conference of high-level officials such as heads of government.

Set-up time
The time needed to arrange, or rearrange after a previous function, the necessary facilities for the next event.

Symposium
This is similar to a seminar except that it is normally concerned with a single subject and the occasion is usually less formal since the flow of information is two-way. It is most common in academic spheres.

Syndicate
See breakout session.

Trade show
A gathering for a trade or competitive exhibition, often with accompanying social events, a conference or workshops and entertainment, which is not open to the general public.

Workshop
A small gathering of people to discuss a specific topic, to exchange ideas or to solve a particular problem (see also Seminar).

Appendix 1

Growth of the UK conference market

Data to analyse whether the UK conference market has grown since the 1990 Coopers and Lybrand Deloitte survey was taken from the continuing sequence of public room sales data produced by BDO. This was extrapolated and subjected to the removal of inflation. The resulting figures give a notional indication of increase.

Source: Public Room Sales Data: BDO *UK Hotel Industry* annual reports.

1989	£479 000	(1989 used as the base year since the 1990
1990	£329 000	Coopers and Lybrand Deloitte report would
1991	£473 000	probably have used 1989 data).
1992	£487 000	
1993	£570 000 ★	
1994	£610 000 ★	
1995	£678 000 ★	

These figures cannot be taken at face value and must be indexed for inflation (Yamane, 1968). This is done by a weighted relative price index:

$$\frac{P1}{PO} = iI \quad \text{where: PO} - 1989 \text{ RPI } 115.2, \text{ and Pi} - 1990 \text{ RPI } 126.1$$

★These data are no longer shown separately in the published reports. For details of the method for weighted relative price indexes see Yamane, T. (1968) *Statistics; An Introductory Analysis*, Harper, New York, 2nd edn, pp. 265–267.

1989	115.2	100	After inflation removed	£479 000
1990	126.1	109.5		£300 456
1991	133.5	115.9		£408 110
1992	138.5	120.2		£405 158
1993	140.7	122.1		£466 830
1994	144.1	125		£488 000
1995	149.1	129		£525 581

Thus, allowing for inflation, there appears to have been a 9.73 per cent increase in public room sales between 1989 and 1995, possibly indicating increased demand, and assuming static room hire rates after inflation.

Assuming the Coopers and Lybrand Deloitte statement of the 1990 (1989) market to be worth 'considerably in excess of £6 billion' to equate to £6.5 billion for calculation purposes, the outcome of a 9.73 per cent increase would be of the order of £7.1 billion. This simply illustrates an increase and should not be inferred as being the actual figure.

The same approach on 115 million delegate days gives a *notional* outcome of 126.2 million delegate days.

Appendix 2 ⸻

Organizations in the conference business ⸻

All phone and fax numbers are given from the UK.

Conference professional bodies

Meeting Industry Association
34 High Street
Broadway
Worcs
WR12 7DT
Tel: 01386 858572
Fax: 01386 858986

Association of British Professional Conference Organisers
The Old Priory
24 High Street
Needingworth, Huntingdon PE17 2SA
Tel & Fax: 01480 496603

Association for Conferences & Events
Riverside House
High Street
Huntingdon, Cambs PE18 6SG
Tel: 01480 457595
Fax: 01480 412863

Incentive Travel and Meetings Association
PO Box 195
Twickenham TW1 2PE
Tel: 0181 892 0256
Fax: 0181 891 3855

Corporate Hospitality Association
Arena House
66–68 Pentonville Road
London
N1 9HS
Tel: 0171 278 0288
Fax: 0171 837 5326

British Exhibition Venues Association
Mallards, Five Ashes
Mayfield, East Sussex
TN20 6NN
Tel: 01435 872244
Fax: 01435 872696

Interpreters

International Association of Conference Interpreters
1 Sandy Road
London NW3 7EY
Tel & Fax: 0181 458 3829

Production Associations and Systems

International Visual Communications
Association Limited
Bolsover House
5/6 Clipstone Street
London W1P 8LD
Tel: 0171 580 0962

Security

British Security Industry Association
Security House
Barbourne Road
Worcester WR1 1RS
Tel: 01905 21464

Conference Placement Agencies

Hotel Booking Agents Association
c/o Booking Service International
BSI House
Blackbrook
Park Avenue
Taunton
TA1 2PF
Tel: 01823 444440

Conference venues: Principal sources of information

British Association of Conference Destinations
1st Floor, Elizabeth House 22 Suffolk Street
Queensway, Birmingham B1 1LS
Tel: 0121 616 1400
Fax: 0121 616 1354

European Federation of Conference Towns
BP 182, 1040 Brussels
Belgium
Tel: 00 322 7326954
Fax: 00 322 7354840

British Tourist Authority Convention and Incentives Division
Thames Tower, Black's Road
Hammersmith
London W6 9EL
Tel: 0181 563 3253
Fax: 0181 563 0302

Higher Education Accommodation Consortium
The Work Station
15 Paternoster Row
Sheffield S1 2BX
Tel: 0114 249 3090
Fax: 0114 249 3091

British Universities Accommodation Consortium
Box No 1389, University Park
Nottingham NG7 2RD
Tel: 0115 950 4571
Fax: 0115 942 2505

International Congress and Convention Association
UK Committee Honorary Secretary
137 Sheen Road
Richmond
Surrey, TW9 1YS

National Convention Bureaux

England – See British Tourist Authority Convention and Incentives Division.

Scottish Convention Bureau
23 Ravelston Terrace
Edinburgh
EH4 3EU
Tel: 0131 332 2433
Fax: 0131 343 1513

Wales Tourist Board Business Travel Dept.
Brunel House
2 Fitzallan Road
Cardiff
CF2 1KY
Tel: 01222 499909
Fax: 01222 48503

Northern Ireland Convention Bureau
St Annes Court
59 North Street
Belfast
BT1 1ND
Tel: 01232 231 221
Fax: 01232 240960

Bord Failte Eireann Convention Bureau
Baggot Street Bridge
Dublin 2
Tel: 00 353 1 602 4000
Fax: 00 353 1 676 4764

Index _____